Pride and
Prejudice

A Study in
Artistic
Economy

TWAYNE'S MASTERWORK STUDIES
ROBERT LECKER, GENERAL EDITOR

ADVENTURES OF HUCKLEBERRY FINN: AMERICAN COMIC VISION
  by *David E. E. Sloane*
ANIMAL FARM: PASTORALISM AND POLITICS by *Richard I. Smyer*
THE BIBLE: A LITERARY STUDY by *John H. Gottcent*
THE BIRTH OF TRAGEDY: A COMMENTARY by *David Lenson*
THE CANTERBURY TALES: A LITERARY PILGRIMAGE by *David Williams*
DUBLINERS: A PLURALISTIC WORLD by *Craig Hansen Werner*
GREAT EXPECTATIONS: A NOVEL OF FRIENDSHIP by *Bert G. Hornback*
HEART OF DARKNESS: SEARCH FOR THE UNCONSCIOUS by *Gary Adelman*
THE INTERPRETATION OF DREAMS: FREUD'S THEORIES REVISITED
  by *Laurence M. Porter*
INVISIBLE MAN: RACE AND IDENTITY by *Kerry McSweeney*
JANE EYRE: PORTRAIT OF A LIFE by *Maggie Berg*
MIDDLEMARCH: A NOVEL OF REFORM by *Bert G. Hornback*
MOBY-DICK: ISHMAEL'S MIGHTY BOOK by *Kerry McSweeney*
ONE FLEW OVER THE CUCKOO'S NEST: RISING TO HEROISM
  by *M. Gilbert Porter*
PARADISE LOST: IDEAL AND TRAGIC EPIC by *Francis C. Blessington*
THE RED BADGE OF COURAGE: REDEFINING THE HERO by *Donald B. Gibson*
THE SCARLET LETTER: A READING by *Nina Baym*
SONS AND LOVERS: A NOVEL OF DIVISION AND DESIRE by *Ross C Murfin*
THE SUN ALSO RISES: A NOVEL OF THE TWENTIES by *Michael S. Reynolds*
TO THE LIGHTHOUSE: THE MARRIAGE OF LIFE AND ART
  by *Alice van Buren Kelley*
THE WASTE LAND: A POEM OF MEMORY AND DESIRE by *Nancy K. Gish*

PRIDE AND PREJUDICE

A STUDY IN ARTISTIC ECONOMY

Kenneth L. Moler

Twayne Publishers
An Imprint of Simon & Schuster Macmillan
NEW YORK

Prentice Hall International
LONDON MEXICO CITY NEW DELHI
SINGAPORE SYDNEY TORONTO

Pride and Prejudice: A Study in Artistic Economy
Kenneth L. Moler

Twayne's Masterwork Studies No. 21

Copyright 1989 by G. K. Hall & Co.
All rights reserved.
Twayne Publishers
An Imprint of Simon & Schuster Macmillan
1633 Broadway,
New York, New York 10019-6785

Book production and design by Gabrielle B. McDonald
Copyediting supervised by Barbara Sutton
Typeset in 10/14 Sabon
by Compset, Inc., Beverly, Massachusetts

Library of Congress Cataloging–in–Publication Data

Moler, Kenneth L.
    Pride and prejudice / Kenneth L. Moler.
      p.   cm. — (Twayne's masterwork studies ; 21)
    Bibliography: p.
    Includes index.
    ISBN 0-8057-7983-3.   ISBN 0-8057-8032-7 (pbk.)
    1. Austen, Jane, 1775–1817. Pride and prejudice. I. Title.
II. Series: Twayne's masterwork studies ; no. 21.
PR4034.P72M64   1988   88-16335
823'.7—dc19   CIP

—— CONTENTS

NOTE ON REFERENCES AND ACKNOWLEDGMENTS
CHRONOLOGY: JANE AUSTEN'S LIFE
AND WORKS

1. Historical Context   1
2. The Importance of the Work   5
3. Critical Reception   8

A READING

4. The Preface: What Austen Does
   Not Deal With   17
5. The Theme of Moral Blindness
   and Self-Knowledge   22
6. The Theme of Art and Nature   35
7. Symbolic Motifs and
   "Conversation Scenes"   50
8. Verbal Styles   63
9. Literary Allusion   81

NOTES   101
BIBLIOGRAPHY   103
INDEX   108
ABOUT THE AUTHOR   110

NOTE ON
REFERENCES
AND ACKNOWLEDGMENTS

The text of *Pride and Prejudice* used for this study is that of the Oxford edition of Jane Austen's works, edited by R. W. Chapman (London: Oxford University Press, 1933), volume 2. References to Austen's *Minor Works* are to volume 6 (1954) of this edition; those to Austen's letters are to *Jane Austen's Letters to Her Sister Cassandra and Others* (London: Oxford University Press, 1952), also edited by Chapman. All page references to Austen's writings are included parenthetically in the text.

The material on Adam Smith's *Theory of Moral Sentiments* used in chapter 7 appeared in my "The Bennett Girls and Adam Smith on Vanity and Pride," *Philological Quarterly* 46 (1967):567–69. Portions of chapter 9 have previously been published in different forms in my *Jane Austen's Art of Allusion* (Lincoln: University of Nebraska Press, 1968, 1977) and in *"Pride and Prejudice*: Jane Austen's Patrician Hero," *Studies in English Literature* 7 (1967):491–508. Part of the material on the title of *Pride and Prejudice* in the chapter on verbal styles appeared in *Persuasions* 8 (1986):25. The portrait of Austen used as a frontispiece, unfortunately the only authentic one, is by Austen's sister Cassandra and is reproduced with permission of the National Portrait Gallery, London.

Jane Austen
1775–1817
Portrait by her sister Cassandra
Courtesy of the National Portrait Gallery, London

CHRONOLOGY: JANE AUSTEN'S LIFE AND WORKS

1775   Birth of Jane Austen, 16 December. She is seventh of the eight children of George Austen, rector of Steventon, Hampshire, and Cassandra (Leigh) Austen. Siblings are James (1765–1819), who becomes a clergyman; George (1766–1838), mentally and/or physically handicapped, about whom almost nothing is known; Edward (1768–1852), adopted by wealthy landowners Mr. and Mrs. Thomas Knight; Henry (1771–1850), who, after military and business careers, becomes a clergyman; Cassandra (1773–1865); Francis (1774–1865) and Charles (1779–1852), both of whom have distinguished careers as naval officers. Beginning of revolution in England's American colonies. Sheridan, *The Rivals*.

1776   Adam Smith, *The Wealth of Nations*.

1778   Fanny Burney, *Evelina*.

1780   Samuel Johnson, *Lives of the Poets*.

1781   Jean-Jacques Rousseau, *Confessions*.

1783–1785   Attends, with Cassandra, schools at Oxford and Southampton (where Jane is critically ill with "putrid fever") and the Abbey School at Reading.

1786   Continues education, directed largely by family, at home. Learns French and Italian, reads extensively in English literature, studies piano.

1789   French Revolution.

1790   Writes *Love and Freindship* [*sic*], a burlesque of romantic fiction. Edmund Burke, *Reflections on the Revolution in France*.

1791	Writes *The History of England,* spoofing Oliver Goldsmith's *History.*
1792	Thomas Paine, *The Rights of Man;* Mary Wollstonecraft, *A Vindication of the Rights of Women.*
1793	England enters war against France. William Godwin, *Political Justice.*
1794	Working on *Lady Susan,* an abortive novel in letters. The Comte de Feuillide, husband of Austen's cousin, is guillotined in France. Ann Radcliffe, *The Mysteries of Udolpho.*
1796–1798	Working on *First Impressions,* prototype of *Pride and Prejudice; Elinor and Marianne,* prototype of *Sense and Sensibility;* and *Susan,* prototype of *Northanger Abbey.*
1797	Cassandra's fiancé dies.
1798	Wordsworth and Coleridge, *Lyrical Ballads.*
1801	Rev. Austen retires, and Jane and Cassandra move to Bath with their parents. Jane is said to have fainted upon hearing of the decision to move. Apparently becomes emotionally involved with a man met while vacationing at Sidmouth, who dies shortly thereafter. Maria Edgeworth, *Castle Rackrent.*
1802	Receives proposal from Harris Bigg-Wither. Accepts, only to change her mind overnight and decline the next morning. Peace of Amiens. Walter Scott, *Minstrelsy of the Scottish Border.*
1803	Sells manuscript of *Susan* to a publisher, who never brings it out. (She is later to buy the manuscript back.) England resumes war with France.
1804	Working on manuscript of *The Watsons,* a novel never completed. Napoleon emperor of France.
1805	Rev. Austen dies. Battle of Trafalgar establishes England as world's supreme naval power.
1806	Moves, with mother and sister, to Southampton.
1807	Abolition of slave trade.
1808	Beginning of Peninsular War.
1809	Moves with family to cottage at Chawton, Hampshire, provided by brother Edward and part of his Hampshire estate.
1811	*Sense and Sensibility* published. Luddite Riots lead to passing of Frame Breaking Bill in 1812.
1812	Napoleon invades Russia. War of 1812 in America.
1813	*Pride and Prejudice* published

Chronology: Jane Austen's Life and Works

1814   *Mansfield Park* published. Scott, *Waverley*.

1815   Invitation by Prince Regent to dedicate *Emma* to him. Battle of Waterloo.

1816   *Emma* published. Scott reviews Austen for *Quarterly Review.*

1817   *Persuasion* completed. Working on manuscript of *Sanditon*, never to be finished. Seriously ill with Addison's disease, moves to Winchester for treatment. Dies, 18 July. Keats, *Poems*.

1818   Posthumous publication of *Persuasion* and *Northanger Abbey*.

1

HISTORICAL CONTEXT

The Intellectual Context

Jane Austen's immediate intellectual milieu is perhaps best described in terms of the title of a recent study of her novels. The period of the late eighteenth and early nineteenth centuries in England is the time of a "a war of ideas," on both the aesthetic and the political and social fronts (the "fronts" are not easily separable in this era). In the first place, there is the Romantic Movement. The earlier neoclassical aesthetic that revered tradition and the "rules" of artistic craftsmanship and that favored man's social existence as the subject matter for art was rejected in the theory and practice of, for example, Wordsworth and Coleridge. It was replaced by one that valued innovation, spontaneity, and individual personal inspiration and that introduced external nature as artistic subject matter of primary importance. "All good poetry," according to the famous passage from the 1800 *Preface to the Lyrical Ballads*, "is the spontaneous overflow of powerful feelings," and these feelings are quite likely to be induced by the sublime, the picturesque, and the beautiful in nature. In the realms of social and political thinking there is the controversy, fanned into flame by the French Revolution abroad and by changing social awareness and economic and social change at home, between followers of what I have elsewhere called the "romantic-revolutionary" school of thought and conservative and anti-Jacobin writers.[1] The romantic-revolution-aries—the school of Rousseau, Tom Paine, William Godwin, Mary Wollstonecraft, Mary Hays, and others—are progressive and demo-cratic in their social and political views. Essentially optimistic regard-ing human nature, they trust the individual heart and mind, and they resist laws, customs, and institutions that inhibit man's "natural" im-pulses. "There is but one power," Godwin writes in *Political Justice,* "to which I can yield a heart-felt obedience, the decision of my own understanding, the dictates of my own conscience." And the impulses of the (uncorrupted) heart, as well as the convictions of the indepen-dent mind, are opposed to the archaic laws and conventions of society in Rousseau's *Nouvelle Héloise* and the novels of Wollstonecraft and Hays. Writers such as Hannah More, Elizabeth Hamilton, and the editors of the *Anti-Jacobin Review,* on the other hand, are conserva-tive in their views on social questions, Burkean in their support of traditional, external authority over untrammelled individualism, skep-tical regarding the goodness of untutored human nature, and often scared witless by the consequences of the revolution in France. The editors of the *Anti-Jacobin* come on strongly in favor of "general and fundamental rules which experience, and wisdom, and justice, and the common consent of mankind, have established," and they react with what seems at times almost paranoiac shrillness to anything tainted with individualistic "modern philosophy" of the Godwinian sort, as potential incitement to revolution.

There have been two lines of thought regarding Austen's response to the historical milieu of the "war of ideas." One was that there was not any response: that, for better or worse, Austen chose to ignore the turmoil outside her "three or four families in a country village" set-tings and to concentrate instead on the inner lives and personal rela-tionships of the kind of people she knew best. This view has been pretty much superseded by a conviction that, while there are no overt polemics in Austen's novels, they are, in subtle but important ways, connected to the social and political and aesthetic issues of her day. That is the view that is taken in this study, and the latter part of chapter 5 will be devoted to expounding it in detail. Austen's response to the late eighteenth-century "war of ideas," I believe, shows her links to some of the great literary figures of the earlier eighteenth century—Johnson, Fielding, Pope—on whose writings she was brought up: for her ultimate position is one of compromise or balance very much in the English Augustan tradition. The demonstration of this point, too, must be reserved for chapter 5 of the reading.

THE LITERARY CONTEXT

The "rise of the novel" in the eighteenth century—I am title borrowing again, this time from Ian Watt's important study of the origins of the novel—presents us with two principal literary modes: those of Samuel Richardson and of Henry Fielding.[2] Richardson's major contribution to the rise of the novel was his deep psychological portrayal of individual human beings. His characters are complex and subtle—enough to make the interpretation of their motivations the source of critical controversy—and we are brought very close to their inner lives. The epistolary technique employed in the novels—the telling of the central characters' stories in letters written by themselves—keeps us within the characters' points of view and creates deep involvement with them. The weakness of the Richardsonian mode, of course, is that it can make it difficult to produce much *more* than interesting psychological portraits. We don't get far enough outside the characters to see them in relation to the kinds of larger issues with which the highest art is concerned. Fielding's novels, on the other hand, with their strong and authoritative omniscient narrators, comment upon and evaluate their materials and achieve a thematic clarity and interest often lacking in Richardson. The obtrusiveness of Fielding's narrators, however, tends to distance us from his characters; the constant sense of an author's presence prevents the kind of intense involvement that is characteristic of our responses to Richardson's protagonists. And Fielding is not very much interested in his characters as individual human beings anyway: Tom Jones and Sophia Western have no "insides" psychologically;

they are, as the narrator is the first to admit, puppets whom he manipulates as he pleases for our instruction and entertainment.

Austen's great achievement in the development of the novel consists in blending the modes of Richardson and Fielding. She uses a narrative point of view that can, and does, relate her characters to important thematic concerns. The narrative "voice" of her novels, however, is very much less obtrusive than that of Fielding's *Tom Jones;* it does not distance us from the characters sufficiently to prevent their being real and interesting to us in and of themselves. And, in the manner of Richardson, Austen presents us with rounded psychological studies: her protagonists lead inner lives of great subtlety and complexity; and, as E. M. Forster remarked, all of her characters are "round, or capable of rotundity." (Actually, what one gets in the Austen novel tends to be a sort of scale of complexity: we move from central characters—Elizabeth and Darcy in *Pride and Prejudice*—of great complexity, to less important figures—Mr. Bennet, Mr. Bingley—who are rounded but not so fully developed, to peripheral figures—Lady Catherine de Bourgh—who approach the flattened out "type" characters of Fielding.) Thus, Austen may be said to have inaugurated what is most nearly the "mainstream" modern novel: the novel that works *through* psychologically developed characters to some sort of larger theme or general vision of life. Appropriately placed chronologically between the eighteenth and nineteenth centuries, she synthesizes the work of her two greatest predecessors of the eighteenth century and opens the door to modern fiction.

2

THE IMPORTANCE OF THE WORK

Why do we continue to read *Pride and Prejudice?* There are, I believe, at least three reasons why Austen's novel has stood the test of time so well. For one thing, there is the technical near-perfection of her work. We experience this on one level in, for instance, the sheer pleasure that comes from seeing the English language so beautifully handled. The narrative voice of the novel, with its crisp precision and at times almost epigrammatic conciseness, is a joy in itself. The dialogues between the intelligent characters—especially the verbal battles of Elizabeth Bennet and Mr. Darcy, of course—delight us with a similar elegance and eloquence. And in the talk of Austen's fools—Mrs. Bennet or Mr. Collins, let us say—we revel in the skill with which various kinds and degrees of mental folly are made to come alive in amusing verbal quirks. Then, as we experience the novel on deeper levels, we come to appreciate the fact that with Austen technical virtuosity is not only a delight per se but also something that "works" with beautiful economy within the larger structural patterns of *Pride and Prejudice.* Not only the handling of language, but the use of low-keyed symbolic motifs (piano playing, libraries, and reading, for instance, as we shall see), the use of various kinds of literary allusions—all of the formal devices of the novel prove, upon inspection, to be highly functional as artistic strategies. It is the almost flawless artistic economy of her writing that is Austen's absolutely undisputed claim to greatness, and the reading of *Pride and Prejudice* that follows will be returning a great many times to this subject.

A second source of Austen's lasting appeal lies in her intense and lively interest in people: in probing character, in analyzing personal relationships, in studying the complex and intriguing business of the moral life. In the two protagonists of *Pride and Prejudice* she gives us a pair of exceedingly "intricate characters," to borrow Elizabeth Bennet's term. Elizabeth and Mr. Darcy are very complicated combinations of high intelligence, discriminating taste, emotional sensitivity, and, on the other hand, a sort of moral blindness regarding themselves and others. And Austen engages us both intellectually and emotionally in their painful progress toward greater self-awareness, toward recognition of their different kinds of pride and prejudice, and thus toward greater perceptiveness regarding those around them. Even the less central characters in the novel are continually suggesting depths that we find ourselves drawn to speculate upon and explore. The relatively minor figure of Charlotte Lucas, for example—the best friend whom Elizabeth, perhaps too hastily, condemns for accepting the fatuous Mr. Collins's proposal of marriage—is a thought-provoking character who elicits an interestingly ambivalent response from the reader. Just how harshly can *we* judge this sexually cool and not very attractive woman's tough-minded decision to marry a man whom she can neither love nor very much respect, and who is marrying her on the rebound from Elizabeth's refusal—how harshly, when we and she know that the alternative is to risk the socially useless and economically dependent old age that may very well be her lot if she does *not* marry Mr. Collins? Or there is Mr. Bennet, whose intelligence and wit—much like those of the narrator of the story and of its heroine— we are attracted to, at the same time that we are repelled by his laziness, cynicism, and lack of responsibility as a father, husband, and landowner. In reading *Pride and Prejudice* we give vigorous and stim-

ulating exercise to our own faculties of moral perception—and, perhaps, like its central characters, grow in the process.

Finally, Austen sees her characters, and encourages the reader to
see them, not only as interesting studies in themselves but also as representatives of the larger intellectual and social currents of her day.
Elizabeth Bennet and Mr. Darcy are very far indeed from being alle-
gorical figures, but considered in the light of the literary-historical
context in which *Pride and Prejudice* exists, they have a good deal to
say to us about the values at stake in the great political, social, and
aesthetic revolutions that marked the latter part of the eighteenth and
the early part of the nineteenth centuries in the Western world. *Pride
and Prejudice,* read with proper historical insight, presents us with a
serious intellectual response to such things as the French and American revolutions, the Romantic Movement in the arts, and the changes
in class structures and relationships taking place in Austen's day. And
it is a response that is relevant to us today; for in *Pride and Prejudice,*
as in all classic literature, specific issues and happenings are seen as
manifestations of forces that are eternal elements in the human
condition.

3

CRITICAL RECEPTION ———

Jane Austen was neither a best-selling author nor the recipient of a great deal of critical attention in her own day. She sold well enough: the first edition of *Pride and Prejudice* (about 1,500 copies) was published in January 1813; it sold out, and a second comparatively small one was issued in November. A third edition appeared in 1817. By comparison, however, Walter Scott's novels were selling out in editions of 10,000 copies by 1820. Nevertheless, Austen was highly regarded, even from the beginning, by a limited, rather sophisticated group of readers. She was invited to dedicate her fourth published novel, *Emma*, to the Prince Regent in 1815. Scott reviewed *Pride and Prejudice, Sense and Sensibility*, and *Emma* (neglecting *Mansfield Park*) favorably in the *Quarterly Review* in 1816. He sounds the note that is, alas, to be typical of nineteenth-century responses to her work when he sees it as a simple, admirably realistic portrayal of everyday life enhanced by unusually strong ability at characterization. While "keeping close to common incidents and to such characters as occupy the ordinary walks of life," he says, she nevertheless produces "sketches of spirit and originality. . . . In this class she stands almost alone." From *Pride and Prejudice* he singles out Mr. Bennet and Mr.

Critical Reception

Collins for special praise. There is little or no sensitivity to Austen's irony on levels other than the verbal one—and not much even to that level. He takes completely seriously Elizabeth Bennet's declaration to her sister Jane that it was the splendors of Pemberley, Darcy's country estate, that led to her change of heart regarding him: her ultimate acceptance of Darcy is the result of allowing "her prudence . . . to subdue her prejudice." Archbishop Richard Whately, in another article in the *Quarterly Review* in 1821, repeats Scott's commendations on realism and characterization and adds perceptive remarks on the intellectual quality of her work, crediting her with both moral and social awareness and a subtle but effective didactic intent—remarks that, unfortunately, went almost unnoticed for the rest of the century.

In the years between her death and 1870 sales of the novels—there was a *Bentley's Standard Novels* edition in 1833—were steady but not very large. There is little or no detailed criticism of importance. One should note, however, the critic George Henry Lewes's occasional praise—although he regrets that "she never stirs the deeper emotions—never fills the soul with a noble aspiration or brightens it with a fine idea"—for her technical mastery and "Shakespearean" powers of characterization, in articles in the *Westminster Review* (1852) and *Blackwood's Magazine* (1859). (The comparison with Shakespeare as a delineator of character is standard in nineteenth-century criticism.) The most perceptive bit of nineteenth-century criticism of Austen is a piece by Richard Simpson in the *North British Review* (1870). Simpson, more than any critic previously—and most critics for years to come—recognizes the extent to which an ironic attitude toward her subject matter is central to Austen's art. And he sees her as an incisive critical mind and a judge, as well as a recorder, of the material she presents. "The critical faculty was in her the ground and support of the artistic faculty," he asserts. Simpson further recognizes, more fully than his predecessors and many of his followers, Austen's intense interest in the intricacies of human nature and the moral life: "Each of her characters, like Shakespeare's *Richard II*, plays in one person many people."

Simpson's essay is in part a review of the first book published on Austen, her nephew James Edward Austen-Leigh's *A Memoir of Jane Austen* (1870). The increase in information the *Memoir* provided about her contributed to an increase in interest that, by the early years of the twentieth century, had raised her to the stature of an important literary figure. She was praised by Virginia Woolf and, especially, by E. M. Forster, in whose *Aspects of the Novel* she figures prominently, and she became a middle-brow favorite as well. In 1923 R. W. Chapman published the definitive scholarly edition of the six novels, and his editions of the letters and minor works appeared in 1932. The year 1939 marks the beginning of modern Austen scholarship with the appearance of Mary Lascelles's *Jane Austen and Her Art*, a remarkable book that foreshadows nearly every line that Austen studies have taken since. If I were asked to choose a single, indispensable book for the prospective student of Austen, it would be Lascelles's study.

Since the 1930s Austen criticism has proliferated at an astounding rate and covered a great range of subjects. One of the more controversial of these concerns Austen's basic attitudes toward the world she depicts. The great trailblazers of the earlier part of the century—Chapman, Lascelles, and David Cecil (*Jane Austen*, 1935), for instance—had, unlike most of their nineteenth-century predecessors, perceived and stressed her stance as an ironic critic, and not merely a skillful describer, of her material. To them, however, she is a satirist of social extremes and deviations who is, on the whole, basically positive about the real values and principles of her world. Some more modern critics, on the other hand, have laid great stress on the radical and subversive elements of her thinking and have seen her irony as a tool for far more caustic and embittered criticism. This attitude is exemplified in an article by D. W. Harding entitled "Regulated Hatred: An Aspect of the Work of Jane Austen" (*Scrutiny* 8, [1940]). It is pushed to the limit—and, according to many critics, beyond—in Marvin Mudrick's *Jane Austen: Irony as Defense and Discovery* (1952). Mudrick's extreme emphasis on the radical elements in Austen leads him to dismiss part of *Pride and Prejudice*, and two of the other novels in toto, as work that is insincere, the product of self-delusion, or in other ways untrue to the "real" Austen. Still more recently there has been a tendency, partly in reaction to the theories of Mudrick and others, to reemphasize the traditional and positive sides of Austen. This is the avowed purpose of A. Walton Litz's *Jane Austen: A Study of Her Artistic Development* (1965). My own *Jane Austen's Art of Allusion* (1968), Alaistair Duckworth's *The Improvement of the Estate* (1972), and Stuart Tave's *Some Words of Jane Austen* (1973) are all works that tend to stress what their authors believe to be an essentially positive vision on Austen's part. The issue remains a highly charged one.

Austen's claims to greater intellectual breadth than nineteenth-century criticism allowed her have been forcefully enhanced in the work of several modern literary historians. *Pride and Prejudice,* in particular, is illuminated in a most exciting way by Samuel Kliger's "*Pride and Prejudice* in the Eighteenth-Century Mode" (*University of Toronto Quarterly* 16 [1947]). Kliger's essay studies the novel in relation to the eighteenth-century tendency to discuss ethical, political, and aesthetic subjects in terms of a dialectic involving the extremes of "art" and "nature." In doing so it both reveals the novel's structural compactness and deals a deadly blow to the notion that Austen is unconcerned with the important intellectual currents of her time. Dorothy van Ghent's essay on *Pride and Prejudice* in *The English Novel: Form and Function* (1953) reads the book in terms of eighteenth-century attitudes toward the individual and society. D. D. Devlin's *Jane Austen and Education* (1975) studies all of the novels in relation to educational theories of the period. And Marilyn Butler's *Jane Austen and the War of Ideas* (1976) relates them to the political and social controversies of the "revolutionary" period of the late eighteenth and early nineteenth centuries.

Modern criticism has paid much attention to Austen's handling of language, and impressionistic appreciations in the manner of Virginia Woolf have given way to specific and detailed analysis. Reuben Brower discussed some of the subtleties of the dialogues between Elizabeth and Darcy in the chapter on *Pride and Prejudice* in *The Fields of Light* (1951). The outstanding work in this area is Howard Babb's *Jane Austen's Novels: The Fabric of Dialogue* (1962). Norman Page's *Jane Austen's Language* (1975) runs a very close second.

A consciousness of Austen's novels' relationship to what Lascelles calls "the world of illusion"—to the themes, situations, and character types that are the stock properties of the fiction of her day—has been an important feature of later twentieth-century scholarship. In "A Critical Theory of Jane Austen's Writings, Part I" (*Scrutiny* 10 [1941]), Q. D. Leavis discusses the relationships between *Pride and Prejudice* and Fanny Burney's novel, *Cecilia*. Henrietta Ten Harmsel, in the chapter on *Pride and Prejudice* in *Jane Austen: A Study in Fictional Conventions* (1964), relates the book, along with Austen's other work, to the novels of Samuel Richardson and Fanny Burney. In my *Jane Austen's Art of Allusion*, I have attempted both to describe a conscious and consistent process of manipulation of recognizably conventional materials throughout Austen's work and, in the chapter on *Pride and Prejudice*, to show this process at work on a particular character type derived from eighteenth-century fiction. F. W. Bradbrook's *Jane Austen and Her Predecessors* (1966) is a more general and far-reaching study of her literary relations.

The Austen novel that most lends itself to, and has profited most from, recent feminist criticism is *Mansfield Park*, rather than *Pride and Prejudice*. (Margaret Fowler's "The Feminist Bias of *Pride and Prejudice*," in the *Dalhousie Review* 57 [1977] is a distinguished exception to this generalization.) For work of general interest in this area one might cite David Monaghan's "Jane Austen and the Position of Women," in *Jane Austen in a Social Context* (ed. Monaghan, 1981); Margaret Kirkham's *Jane Austen, Feminism and Fiction* (1983); and LeRoy W. Smith's *Jane Austen and the Drama of Women* (1983).

Austen is now one of the most written-about of all novelists. A steady stream of articles, books, and dissertations makes simply keeping up with the annual Austen bibliography a considerable task for the student of her work. There is a periodical—*Persuasions,* edited by Austen scholar Gene Koppel for the Jane Austen Society of North America—devoted exclusively to Austen studies. The writer who began as more or less a succès d'estime has become a veritable scholarly industry. On the popular front, she has been issued in countless paperback editions, translated into just about every language you can think of, filmed, and televised. And the trends, both scholarly and popular, show no signs of abating. One can purchase a two-volume, annotated bibliography of Jane Austen studies, produced by the University Press of Virginia, which runs to a total of 631 pages and covers only the years from 1952 to 1973. One can also invest in a Jane Austen T-shirt if so inclined, or adorn one's car with a bumper sticker that proclaims, "I'd rather be reading Jane Austen."

a reading

4

THE PREFACE:
WHAT AUSTEN
DOES NOT DEAL WITH

Know then thyself, presume not God to scan;
The proper study of Mankind is Man.

Pope, *Essay on Man*, Epistle 2

One of the things that one must come to terms with in trying to appreciate Austen's art is what she does not write about. She does not deal with Ultimate Questions: who are we, why are we here, what does it all mean? For her, the answers to such questions as these are contained, for the purposes of her art anyway, within the pages of the catechism. Her characters do plenty of soul-searching, as the following chapters illustrate. But their soul-searching is not about what the meanings and purposes of their lives are, much less about what the meaning of Life is. They are attempting, not to "find" themselves, as so many characters in modern literature are, but to "know" themselves, in the sense in which the couplet from Pope quoted above uses the term. Jane Austen's novels confine themselves to the moral and social realms: they "presume not God to scan."

This is, for some twentieth-century readers, a serious limitation of her writing. Many of us cut our critical teeth on the cosmic pessimism of Hardy, on Conrad's and Golding's probings into the heart of darkness, on the spiritual quests of Dostoyevski's characters, on George Eliot's, D. H. Lawrence's, and E. M. Forster's attempts to find ground on which to base a life in the absence of traditional Christian belief. When we do not find Austen dealing with similar things, we may tend to depreciate her art accordingly. Even so fine a critic as Dorothy Van Ghent seems to feel that *Pride and Prejudice* needs to be pardoned for a certain lack of profundity: "It is wronging an Austen novel to expect of it what it makes no pretense to rival—the spiritual profundity of the very greatest novels. But if we expect artistic mastery of limited materials, we shall not be disappointed.[3]

Readers of *Pride and Prejudice* should try to divest themselves of the kind of twentieth-century conditioning I have been describing, because Austen's novel, rightly read, is just as "profound" as *Lord Jim* or *The Idiot* or *A Passage to India* (and considerably more profound than *Lady Chatterley's Lover* or *Lord of the Flies*). There are at least two considerations that may be of use in enabling one to approach *Pride and Prejudice* in the most rewarding way.

The first of these is that it surely makes some critical sense to try to look at the novel, at least initially, in the light of its own literary traditions rather than ours. Although Austen's novels were not published until the nineteenth century, her intellectual roots are sunk deep in eighteenth-century neoclassicism. One of the very strongest features of neoclassic thought is the belief that it is not man's business to speculate about metaphysical questions, and not within his capacity to do so profitably. The Age of Reason actually took a rather dim view of man's capacity for complicated and abstract reasoning. It also felt that, fortunately, such reasoning was not necessary. The few ultimate truths we need to carry on life with are simple and available to the normal man's common sense. The literary historian Arthur O. Lovejoy has labeled this belief "rationalistic anti-intellectualism": "the presumption of the universal accessibility and verifiability of all that it is really needful for man to know (and) that all subtle, elaborate, intricate reasonings about abstruse questions beyond the grasp of the majority are certainly unimportant, and probably untrue.[4]

Virtually all of the eighteenth century's greatest writers share this presumption and display it in both theory and practice. Jonathan Swift's admirable Brobdignagians, in *Gulliver's Travels*, Book 2, confine their educational system to "morality, history, poetry, and (applied) mathematics" and cannot grasp the importance of "ideas, entities, abstractions and transcendentals." There are not more than one thousand volumes in the Royal Library of Brobdignag. The even more exemplary Houyhnhnms of Book 4 restrict their learning to the same subjects and do not even need writing to carry on their culture. In contrast to these model civilizations are those of Book 3: Laputa, the flying island whose absurd inhabitants devote their lives to abstruse speculation, or Balnibarbi, with its academy devoted to complicated and useless "scientific" projects. According to the wise Imlac, in Samuel Johnson's *Rasselas*, "truth, such as is necessary to the regulation of life, is always found where it is honestly sought," and the mad astronomer Rasselas encounters in his travels is a monument to the folly of too much abstract speculation. In Epistle 1 of the *Essay on Man* when Pope *must* touch upon metaphysics, he concentrates on establishing a few fundamental and (to him) self-evident and universally accepted truths and, after much caution regarding the fatal "pride" of attempting to go beyond them, polishes off the topic with the couplet with which this preface began and devotes the rest of the *Essay* to the ethical and social realms. All of the best neoclassical poetry (Dryden's *Absalom and Achitophel, The Medal, MacFlecknoe,* for example, Pope's *Rape of the Lock, Dunciad,* Moral Epistles) derives from these latter realms. The great founders of the eighteenth-century novel—Fielding and Richardson—are concerned with defining and rewarding moral virtue, with social commentary, and with (in the case of Richardson) delicate and difficult social and personal relationships.

This is the literary tradition in which *Pride and Prejudice* is rooted, and most literate people think it produced its share of great work. We ought to approach Austen's novel thinking not of nineteenth- and twentieth-century models, but of the cultural traditions of the eighteenth century. Most of us are willing to make considerable temporary intellectual adjustments in order to understand and enjoy Chaucer and Shakespeare and Milton. Because Austen's characters and language are not so obviously the product of alien cultures, we may be less inclined to make similar imaginative adjustments on her behalf. But they are necessary. Fitzwilliam Darcy's and Elizabeth Bennet's world is not that of Joyce's Stephen Dedalus or Lawrence's Ursula Brangwen—nor even that of Hardy's Jude or Eliot's Maggie Tolliver: it is closer to that of Fielding's Tom Jones and Pope's Belinda. Not to accept this fact is critically naïve, and it compels us, if we are consistent in our naïveté, to find Dryden, Pope, Swift, Johnson, Fielding, Richardson, and a number of other rather highly regarded writers, as well as Austen, lamentably "limited" compared to ourselves.

A second thing that we might profitably consider is whether it is really sensible or useful (or possible) to set up a sort of hierarchy as far as the subject matter of art is concerned: to give most critical "points" to works dealing with metaphysics, fewer to those dealing with social criticism, still fewer to those concerned with ethics and personal relations, and so on. Assuming that we could agree on an order of priorities (and of course we could not—Marxist and other politically oriented critics obviously would not go along with the order above, for instance) would we not still find ourselves in a rather embarrassing critical position? Logically, we would have to say that Shakespeare's finest comedy—or most magnificent sonnet—is somehow intrinsically inferior to one of his best tragedies, since it does not deal with the same kinds of philosophical themes. Is it inferior, or does it simply possess a different kind, rather than degree, of excellence? We do, most of us, demand some sort of intellectual and/or emotional profundity from the works we call *great*—some sense that our minds have been enlarged, our emotional capacities expanded, that we have "grown" by reading them. But does this profundity not derive far more from an artist's handling of his subject matter than from the subject matter itself? Golding's *Lord of the Flies* deals with what one must call a very "profound" question—the problem of evil, in fact—but deals with it in a way that for many readers is simplistic and intellectually unsatisfying. Pope's *Rape of the Lock* is a comic treatment of social misconduct in the café society of his day; but the reader who takes a good look at things like the scene where Belinda's dressing-table turns into an altar, or what happens to the word "honor" in the speech made by the shallow socialite Thalestris, comes away from the poem having both thought and felt pretty deeply. It seems to me that, as it was for the eighteenth-century writers cited earlier, the moral and social life, profoundly *handled,* is suitable matter for complex, interesting, mind-and-heart expanding art. That is what we get in *Pride and Prejudice,* and that is enough, I think, to make charges of intellectual "limitation" irrelevant.

5

THE THEME OF MORAL BLINDNESS AND SELF-KNOWLEDGE ———

"It is a truth universally acknowledged, that a single man in possession of a good fortune, must be in want of a wife." The sentence with which *Pride and Prejudice* begins is one of the most famous opening lines in literature. The contrast between what it seems to be saying with almost philosophic gravity and the truth of the situation to which it refers—which is that, in fact, in Austen's world, it is poor single women, like the Bennet girls, who are desperately in want of affluent husbands—creates an irony that has been captivating to readers down the generations. Irony of this sort is the characteristic tone of *Pride and Prejudice*. We hear it very frequently in the voice of the narrator. Miss Bingley and Mrs. Hurst, we are told, "had been educated in one of the first private seminaries in town, had a fortune of twenty thousand pounds, were in the habit of spending more than they ought, and of associating with people of rank; and were therefore in every respect entitled to think well of themselves and meanly of others" (15). Charlotte Lucas accepts Mr. Collins's proposal of marriage "solely from the pure and disinterested desire of an establishment" (121). We hear similar irony constantly in the voice of Mr. Bennet, who gets a number of the best lines in the novel and, in many instances (although not always, as we shall see), has his author's approval. And we hear it quite often in the voice of the novel's heroine. One might note parenthetically that irony in various forms is important in all of Austen's work. One entire book and countless scholarly articles have been devoted to this aspect of her work.

The verbal irony that we have been observing so far provides the background for another, larger sort of irony that is built into the very structure of *Pride and Prejudice*. This is the irony that arises from the reader's frequent and amused perception of the discrepancy between what the protagonists of the story, Elizabeth Bennet and Mr. Darcy, *think* about a given person or situation and what we, the audience, know to be the truth. We are constantly seeing Darcy and Elizabeth, highly intelligent and sensitive and articulate as they are, making the most fundamental sorts of errors in judgment about their fellow human beings. We, for instance, know that, in the early part of the story, Elizabeth would consider Darcy about as eligible as Varney the Vampire as a prospective marriage partner. Darcy, however, after a few days in her company, is perfectly convinced that if he could condescend to propose to her she would jump at the chance to marry him and only fears lest some word or look of his may have given grounds to "elevate her with the hope of influencing his felicity." Thus arises the delightful scene where, on the last day of Elizabeth's visit at Mr. Bingley's house, Darcy (having carefully avoided speaking to her all day) feels it necessary to bury his nose in a book when they are left alone together by chance for half an hour.

> Elizabeth had been at Netherfield long enough. She attracted him more than he liked—and Miss Bingley was uncivil to *her*, and more teazing than usual to himself. He wisely resolved to be particularly careful that no sign of admiration should *now* escape him, nothing that could elevate her with the hope of influencing his felicity; sensible that if such an idea had been suggested, his behaviour during the last day must have material weight in confirming or crushing it. Steady to his purpose, he scarcely spoke ten words to her through

the whole of Saturday, and though they were at one time left by themselves for half an hour, he adhered most conscientiously to his book, and would not even look at her. (60)

With somewhat more justification, perhaps, Darcy fails to understand the nature and strength of Jane Bennet's feelings for his friend Bingley—he sees, wants to see her, as being interested in the match more than the man—and glosses over the depth of the relationship between Jane and Bingley.

Elizabeth also has her share of failures in perceptiveness. She prides herself on being a "studier of character," as Mr. Bingley calls her, but how well does she really know her very good friend Charlotte Lucas, for example? When Charlotte agrees to marry the dull, pompous, physically unattractive but well-heeled Mr. Collins, Elizabeth responds with amazement and horror. Yet we—and she as well—have frequently heard Charlotte's worldly-wise if not actually mercenary endorsements of marriage for a comfortable establishment rather than for love. And we see, although Elizabeth will not, that, after Elizabeth has turned Mr. Collins down, Charlotte is doing everything in her power to capture him for herself:

> The Bennets were engaged to dine with the Lucases, and again during the chief of the day, was Miss Lucas so kind as to listen to Mr. Collins. Elizabeth took the opportunity of thanking her. "It keeps him in good humour," said she, "and I am more obliged to you than I can express." Charlotte assured her friend of her satisfaction in being useful, and that it amply repaid her for the little sacrifice of her time. This was very amiable, but Charlotte's kindness extended farther than Elizabeth had any conception of;—its object was nothing less, than to secure her from any return of Mr. Collins's addresses, by engaging them towards herself. (121)

Charlotte, not much interested in men and very much interested in marriage as her only preservative from a prospective nearly penniless spinsterhood, is both consistent and undisguised in her sexual maneuverings for Collins. But Elizabeth cannot see or accept this. Shrewd as she can be in analyzing character in many instances, she is woefully mistaken in her own best friend.

Again, Elizabeth is completely taken in by the almost transparent duplicity of Mr. Wickham regarding himself and his relations with Mr. Darcy and the Darcy family. The story of persecution and injustice at Darcy's hands that Wickham tells Elizabeth at Mrs. Phillips's party (76–82) is clearly fishy. To begin with, Wickham contradicts himself, declaring that he will never expose Darcy's conduct publicly, because of his respect and affection for Darcy's father, when in fact he is doing just that in telling it to Elizabeth. And is it not extremely suspicious—especially given early nineteenth-century English standards of personal reticence—that a gentleman should spill out the details of the most painful episodes of his life to a near-stranger in what is in effect their first conversation? Wickham's later conduct is even more revealing. Although he has declared to Elizabeth that he will not attempt to avoid meeting Darcy in public, it is he, not Darcy, who fails to show up at the ball given at Netherfield by Mr. Bingley where they would have been thrown together. And as soon as Darcy leaves the vicinity we learn that Wickham is assiduously spreading throughout the neighborhood the story he has vowed to Elizabeth to conceal (138). All of this Elizabeth realizes in the moments of revelation that follow her reading of Darcy's letter after his unsuccessful proposal to her:

> She was *now* struck with the impropriety of such communications to a stranger, and wondered it had escaped her before. She saw the indelicacy of putting himself forward as he had done, and the inconsistency of his professions with his conduct. She remembered that he had boasted of having no fear of seeing Mr. Darcy—that Mr. Darcy might leave the country, but that *he* should stand his ground; yet he had avoided the Netherfield ball the very next week. She remembered also, that till the Netherfield family had quitted the country, he had told his story to no one but herself; but that after their removal, it had been every where discussed; that he had then no reserve, no scruples in sinking Mr. Darcy's character, though he had assured her that respect for the father, would always prevent his exposing the son. (206–7)

But we have—and Elizabeth should have—known all of this long before.

Most important, of course, is Elizabeth's misjudgment of Darcy's character: the overreaction to his pride and reserve that makes her unable to see what lies beneath it. This leads, in the earlier parts of the novel, to many amusing bits of dialogue where Elizabeth and Darcy talk at cross-purposes. There is the scene at Sir William Lucas's party where Sir William attempts to persuade Elizabeth and Darcy to dance together and Elizabeth refuses Darcy's invitation:

[Sir William] was struck with the notion of doing a very gallant thing, and called out to her,

"My dear Miss Eliza, why are you not dancing?—Mr. Darcy, you must allow me to present this young lady to you as a very desirable partner.—You cannot refuse to dance, I am sure, when so much beauty is before you." And taking her hand, he would have given it to Mr. Darcy, who, though extremely surprised, was not unwilling to receive it, when she instantly drew back. . . .

"You excel so much in the dance, Miss Eliza, that it is cruel to deny me the happiness of seeing you; and though this gentleman dislikes the amusement in general, he can have no objection, I am sure, to oblige us for one half hour."

"Mr. Darcy is all politeness," said Elizabeth, smiling. (26)

Darcy, as we have been told, is by now considerably interested in Elizabeth and would really rather like to dance with her. Elizabeth's refusal, with its snide "Mr. Darcy is all politeness" (i.e., Mr. Darcy need not martyr himself to the common forms of politeness on *her* account) misreads him and his real feelings about her. Again, when Elizabeth is visiting at Netherfield in order to nurse her sister Jane, and Miss Bingley and Mrs. Hurst are entertaining the company with music one evening, Miss Bingley includes a "lively Scotch air" in the program. Darcy asks Elizabeth if this does not make her feel inclined to dance, and Elizabeth is instantly upon the defensive:

"Do not you feel a great inclination, Miss Bennet, to seize such an opportunity of dancing a reel?"
She smiled, but made no answer. He repeated the question, with some surprise at her silence.
"Oh!" said she, "I heard you before; but I could not immediately determine what to say in reply. You wanted me, I know, to say yes, that you might have the pleasure of despising my taste; but I always delight in overthrowing those kind of schemes, and cheating a person of their premeditated contempt. I have therefore made up my mind to tell you, that I do not want to dance a reel at all—and now despise me if you dare."
"Indeed I do not dare." (52)

Overly sensitive on the subject of dancing where Darcy is concerned and anxious to show that, unlike her rowdy younger sisters, she is not eager to seize all possible opportunities of dancing anything at all, she responds to his question on the assumption that it is a form of insult. As his gallant, almost flirtatious replies show, however, his motives have been quite different. The question may have been semiserious, or it may have been designed as a conversational "opener," but it certainly was framed with a desire to please rather than with a wish to insult. On yet another occasion, when Elizabeth performs on the pianoforte at Rosings, Lady Catherine de Bourgh's house, Darcy rather conspicuously leaves Lady Catherine's side to come and listen to Elizabeth (173–76). Elizabeth assumes that he comes in an attitude of supercilious criticism and attacks him accordingly: "You mean to frighten me, Mr. Darcy, by coming in all this state to hear me? But I will not be alarmed, though your sister *does* play so well." Actually, Darcy's move can arise from one or both of two motives: he may wish to put a stop, out of consideration for Elizabeth's feelings, to the gross rudeness of his aunt, who is talking aloud to him in the midst of Elizabeth's performance; or he may be moved by a genuine desire to listen to—and look at—Elizabeth. (And is the desire spurred, in this case, by a spot of sexual jealousy? Elizabeth is, and has been, giving a good deal of her time and attention to the very attractive and charming Colonel Fitzwilliam, for whom she is chiefly playing in this scene, and who has taken "a chair near her" on the occasion.) At any rate Darcy's action stems from feelings quite different from those that Elizabeth, in her hostile state of mind, attributes to him.

But these minor misunderstandings are only small manifestations of Elizabeth's more crucial misjudgment of Darcy's basic character, the error upon which the plot of the novel turns. The major "action" of the story, once Elizabeth has put down Darcy's pride by her angry refusal of his proposal of marriage, concerns her recognition of her wrong-headedness regarding him and her reevaluation of the man she has scorned. She must learn that in her own kind of pride and prejudice she has "courted prepossession and ignorance" regarding Darcy. She must learn to see the solid moral worth, the intelligence, and the sensitivity that make him alone among the cast of characters of *Pride and Prejudice* her moral equal. She must move from the image of him as merely the proud, pompous, and prejudiced patrician to the affirmation: "I love him. Indeed he has no *improper* pride" (376; my italics). This, after all, is what the story is chiefly "about."

One of the main themes of *Pride and Prejudice*, then, concerns a sort of moral blindness on the part of the book's protagonists, a blindness that it is one of the functions of Austen's irony to reveal. Both Elizabeth and Darcy must learn to do a better job of evaluating character and motive. And, in Austen's philosophy, the prerequisite for seeing others clearly is seeing oneself clearly; in other words, attaining self-knowledge.

"There is," Mr. Darcy says to Elizabeth in one of their early arguments, "in every disposition a tendency to some particular evil, a natural defect, which not even the best education can overcome" (58). The conversation becomes humorous, as Elizabeth takes over, but the statement is exceedingly important and lies at the center of Austen's moral vision. The discovery of particular evils and natural defects, of special mental and emotional biases that must be recognized and at least partially overcome before one can attain moral maturity, is a recurring pattern throughout her fiction. Austen is one in a long line of classical and Christian moral thinkers who have seen the attempt to "know thyself" as one of the most important concerns involved in the business of being human. This is hardly surprising, given her intellectual background, education, and temperament. There was a very strong emphasis on self-knowledge in the eighteenth- and early nineteenth-century moral writers whose work made up a substantial part of her (and her audience's) reading. David Hume, Samuel Johnson, Adam Smith—on a lower but more popular level, Dr. Barrows, Thomas Gisbourne, Hannah More—all these and many others are much concerned with what More calls the "faculty of self-inspection" and its functions and its failures. (In 1745 a man named John Mason published a book entitled *Self-Knowledge,* which attained something like the status of a best-seller.) As a practicing Christian, the daughter and sister of clergymen, Austen saw self-examination as an important part of her religious duties. "Teach us to understand the sinfulness of our own hearts," asks a prayer she composed for private use, "and save us from deceiving ourselves by pride or vanity" (*Minor Works,* 453–54). And self-knowledge—the lack of it, the difficult attainment of it, the manifestation of it by those who have achieved it—is central in the moral lives of her protagonists. (Catherine Morland, the heroine of *Northanger Abbey;* Marianne Dashwood, one of the two heroines of *Sense and Sensibility;* Edmund Bertram, the hero of *Mansfield Park;* Emma Woodhouse of *Emma;* and Captain Wentworth of *Persuasion* are all led toward self-knowledge of various kinds in the courses of their stories.)

Elizabeth and Darcy are no exceptions to the rule. Both fail in their judgments of others because of mental and temperamental biases in themselves of which they are initially unaware. Elizabeth misjudges Charlotte Lucas because of the kind of person *Elizabeth* is. Indifferent to monetary and social concerns herself, she will not believe that someone that she cares for could feel differently. She credits Wickham in part because, having pretty strong egalitarian feelings herself and an established dislike for the rank-conscious Darcy, she *wants* to see Wickham as the victim of heartless, overbearing aristocracy. (Although, obviously, temporary sexual attraction to Wickham plays a part here as well.) She is unfair to Darcy because he has become for her the representative of a pride in rank and wealth that runs counter to her own beliefs regarding what is important and valuable in life. On the other hand Darcy's complacency regarding his desirability as a marriage partner, his arrogance, and his doubts about the strength and genuineness of Jane Bennet's feelings for Bingley all stem to a large extent from his tendency to think and feel too much in terms of purely social values: his pride in his own advantages and his prejudice against those who lack a similar background and income.

For Elizabeth the most dramatic step in her progress toward self-knowledge and moral perceptiveness comes with the shock she receives from the letter that Darcy writes to her after his proposal and their quarrel. Reading the letter forces her to see how much she has allowed her pride and prejudice to cloud her judgment, and it fills her with shame for her self-induced obtuseness:

> She grew absolutely ashamed of herself.—Of neither Darcy nor Wickham could she think, without feeling that she had been blind, partial, prejudiced, absurd.
> "How despicably have I acted! she cried.—"I, who have prided myself on my discernment!—I, who have valued myself on my abilities! Who have often disdained the generous candour of my sister, and gratified my vanity, in useless or blameable distrust—How humiliating is this discovery!—Yet, how just a humiliation—Had I been in love, I could not have been more wretchedly blind. But vanity, not love, has been my folly—pleased with the preference of one, and offended by the neglect of the other, on the very beginning of our acquaintance, I have courted prepossession and ignorance, and driven reason away where either were concerned. Till this moment, I never knew myself." (208)

The metaphor of blindness that runs throughout this passage is worth noting, for it recurs throughout Austen's novels in similar scenes of self-revelation. In each of her five other novels at least one central character uses, or is described in terms of, language having to do with vision in such a scene. It was for this reason that, in a work written some years ago, I chose the term "moral blindness" to describe this crucial Austen concern.

The Theme of Moral Blindness and Self-Knowledge

Once Elizabeth has been shocked and humiliated into the knowledge of her moral blindness and its causes, she receives more evidence regarding Darcy's real character and can now evaluate it properly. Very important to her changing perception of Darcy is her visit to his home, Pemberley. For one thing there is, quite simply, the physical appearance of the place and what this implies. Elizabeth—the "pre-letter" Elizabeth anyway—would have expected to find Pemberley very much like Lady Catherine de Bourgh's Rosings Park: an ostentatious display of its owner's status, where magnificence displaces taste and comfort. Actually she finds that Darcy's house and grounds are truly beautiful. They are grand, from scale and natural advantages, but they are not pretentious. They reflect the good sense and excellent taste of its owners, past and present, at every turn. Elizabeth has "never seen a place where natural beauty had been so little counteracted by an awkward taste" (243). Moreover, at Pemberley Elizabeth has an opportunity of hearing an account of Darcy's character from his housekeeper that gives her much food for thought (246–49). He is, as she learns, a competent and caring landlord, well versed in the management of his estates, and respected and well liked by his tenants and dependants. "There is not one of his tenants or servants but what will give him a good name," the housekeeper affirms. And Elizabeth, as she looks at his picture in the course of her tour of Pemberley House, considers a side of him to which she has not given much thought before:

> As a brother, a landlord, a master, she considered how many people's happiness were in his guardianship!—How much of pleasure or pain it was in his power to bestow!—How much of good or evil must be done by him! Every idea that had been brought forward by the housekeeper was favorable to his character, and as she stood before the canvas, on which he was represented, and fixed his eyes upon herself, she thought of his regard with a deeper sentiment of gratitude than it had ever raised before; she remembered its warmth, and softened its impropriety of expression. (250–51)

In addition, Darcy, on his own home grounds, proves to be a thoroughly polite and considerate host, even to the woman who has angrily rejected his proposal of marriage and to those relatives of hers whom he knows to be "in trade in London." At Pemberley, then, Elizabeth discovers in Darcy a discriminating and unaffected taste congenial to her own, a strong sense of duty and social concern that she must admire, and a capacity for unassuming, genuine politeness that is a surprise to her. (Perhaps partly because there was not so much *of* it before? Darcy too has changed by now, as we shall see.) When her sister Jane, learning of Elizabeth's engagement, asks when Elizabeth first began to be aware of her love for Darcy, Elizabeth replies, "I believe I must date it from my first seeing his beautiful grounds at Pemberley" (373). She is joking, of course; but there is a fundamental truth behind the witticism.

Finally, Elizabeth sees Darcy's character manifested in his behavior in the affair between her youngest sister Lydia and Mr. Wickham. The strong sense of responsibility mentioned by his housekeeper is here brought dramatically and personally home to Elizabeth. Darcy believes that is is his duty, because of Wickham's connection with the Darcy family and because of the knowledge of Wickham's real character that he possessed, to undo as far as possible the harm Wickham has done, and he takes the leading part in the business of bullying and bribing Wickham into matrimony. Here, I believe, Austen sets up Mr. Bennet as a sort of foil to Mr. Darcy, and Elizabeth is meant to perceive the contrast between the two men, to her moral advantage. Mr. Bennet, like the daughter who most resembles him in intelligence and temperament, has often been allowed to enjoy himself and amuse the reader with his socially irreverent remarks. Compared with him, Darcy has often appeared ponderous and stuffy. Here, however, social irreverence gets its comeuppance, for its concomitant proves to be social irresponsibility. Mr. Bennet, we know, has never been an adequate head of his family: he has failed to manage his estate in such a way as to accumulate a financial provision for his wife and daughters in the event of his death, and his only contribution to his daughters' education has been to undermine what little authority their air-headed mother has with them. Now, at a climax in his family's fortunes, he proves dramatically ineffectual in the Wickham affair, allows Darcy to settle it for him, and, when Darcy has done so, returns to his library almost untouched by his failures as a husband and father. It is clear, I think, that Elizabeth has always had a strong identification with her father and that her own socially irreverent wit is part of her paternal inheritance. Is it not a part of her growing-up to become less identified with him and to relate more closely to a sense of one's social role that, if it may make for stiffness and stuffiness at times, also ensures the performance of social duty? Her remark to her father that Darcy has "no *improper* pride" marks her partial transfer of allegiance to Darcy's social code and the valuable qualities it can produce. And it sets the seal on her growth into self-knowledge and moral perceptiveness.

Elizabeth Bennet's process of moral growth is played out before our eyes. Fitzwilliam Darcy's, on the other hand, takes place largely offstage, and we are told about it in the scene of his second proposal to Elizabeth (365–69). It appears to follow the same pattern as Elizabeth's, however: a sudden shock to one's pride and preconceptions is followed by a painful self-appraisal and leads to clearer insights into oneself and others. Elizabeth's refusal of his first proposal, with its scathing assessments of his personality and character (he is clearly never going to forget that she once had cause to refer to him as not "gentlemanlike"), is for Darcy what Darcy's letter is for Elizabeth. When he was "reasonable enough to allow the justice" of Elizabeth's criticisms, he says, he saw himself as he really was:

> As a child I was taught what was *right*, but I was not taught to correct my temper. I was given good principles, but left to follow them in pride and conceit. . . . I was spoilt by my parents, who, though good themselves, (my father, particularly, all that was benevolent and amiable) allowed, encouraged, almost taught me to be selfish and overbearing, to care for none beyond my own family circle, to think meanly of all the rest of the world, to *wish* at least to think meanly of their sense and worth compared to my own. Such I was, from eight to eight-and-twenty; and such I might still have been but for you, dearest, loveliest Elizabeth! What do I not

owe you! You taught me a lesson, hard indeed at first, but most advantageous. By you, I was properly humbled. (369)

The acquisition of greater self-knowledge makes Darcy less arrogant and overbearing: he repents of and repairs his interference in the love affair between Jane Bennet and Mr. Bingley. It enables him to see the Gardiner family not simply as the merchants from Cheapside whom he had joined Miss Bingley in scorning but as the worthy, sensible, and well-mannered people they are in themselves, and he welcomes them as frequent visitors to Pemberley "on the most intimate terms." It makes him fit for the deep and mutually rewarding relationship that he and Elizabeth will obviously enjoy—the kind of relationship that Austen bestows on each of her protagonists when he has reached moral maturity.

Pride and Prejudice is, then, first and foremost a story about learning and growth in the complicated and fascinating business of the moral life. Elizabeth and Darcy, when we first encounter them, are, in spite of their obviously high degree of intelligence, profoundly ignorant about important aspects of themselves, and this lack of self-knowledge manifests itself in blindness, sometimes comic but ultimately very serious, regarding others—particularly, of course, regarding one another. They grow, suffering but profitting by it, into self-knowledge in the course of the story, and they demonstrate their growth by the removal of the different kinds of pride and prejudice that had blinded them, and kept them apart, at first. To borrow the words of the popular *Self-Knowledge* of John Mason (vol. 2, chap. 6): "Self-knowledge indeed does not enlarge or increase our natural capacities, but it guides and regulates them; leads us to the right use and application of them; and removes a great many things which obstruct their due exercise; as pride, prejudice, and passion etc., which oftentimes so miserably pervert the rational powers."

6

THE THEME OF ART AND NATURE

Some Backgrounds

A second very important theme in *Pride and Prejudice* concerns what I shall refer to as an "art–nature" dialectic. Some historical background is perhaps desirable before we turn to the various manifestations of this theme in the novel itself. We should begin with the consideration that the eighteenth-century mind is strongly influenced by (among others) two important ideas that it inherits, in considerably diluted forms, from the medieval and Renaissance world pictures.

The first of these is the idea that the creation is ordered as a series of analogous planes, or macrocosms and microcosms. As E. M. W. Tillyard puts it, to the Elizabethan mind the world "consisted of a number of planes, arranged one below the another in order of dignity, but connected by an immense net of correspondence. . . . The different planes were the divine and angelic, the universe or macrocosm, the commonwealth or body politic, man or the microcosm, and the lower creation.⁵ The structures of the higher planes are mirrored in those of the lower, and alterations or aberrations on one plane may affect another level. We see this idea reflected in the familiar medieval and Renaissance analogy between the state and the solar system or the cosmos. The king corresponds to the sun; his rule keeps the various elements in the body politic—which correspond to the planets—in their proper order. One of the most eloquent expressions of this correspondence is found in the famous speech by Ulysses on "degree" in Shakespeare's *Troilus And Cressida* (1, 3):

> The heavens themselves, the planets and this centre
> Observe degree priority and place
> Insisture course proportion season form
> Office and custom, all in line of order;
> And therefore is the glorious planet Sol
> In noble eminence enthron'd and spher'd
> Amidst the other, whose med'cinable eye
> Corrects the ill aspects of planets evil
> And posts like the commandment of a king,
> Sans check, to good and bad. But when the planets
> In evil mixture to disorder wander,
> What plagues and what portents, what mutiny,
> What raging of the sea, shaking of earth,
> Commotion in the winds, frights changes horrors,
> Divert and crack, rend and deracinate
> The unity and married calm of states
> Quite from their fixture. Oh, when degree is shak'd,
> The enterprise is sick.

One might also call to mind the passages in Shakespeare's *Julius Caesar* where upheaval in the heavens is seen as connected with the violation of civil order in the assassination of Caesar and its consequences. Analogies between the mind, or body, or both, of man and the macrocosm above him are equally frequent. To remain with the work of Shakespeare, one might cite the grand speech of Lorenzo to Jessica in *The Merchant of Venice* (5, 1) when, after reflecting upon the glory of a starry night and describing the heavenly harmony that governs the spheres above them, he affirms that "Such harmony is in immortal souls / But while this muddy vesture of decay / Doth grossly clothe it in, we cannot hear it." Lorenzo cites as evidence of the correspondence the effects of music upon the mind. As the work of Tillyard and others has exhaustively shown, the passages cited above are merely particularly effective expressions of ideas that are commonplaces to Shakespeare's generation and those preceding it. To the medieval and Renaissance mind the creation is a Great Chain of Being, an orderly, interconnected hierarchy in which the same general laws apply on all levels.

Second, we should note that one of these great universal laws is the principle known as *concordia discors,* harmonious discord. In the world picture we are considering the universe consists of four basic elements: earth, air, water, and fire. Earth, being cold and dry, is antithetical to air, which is hot and moist. Water, being cold and moist, is antithetical to fire, which is hot and dry. In the chaos preceding creation these elements were perpetually at war with one another. God created cosmos from chaos by balancing the antithetical elements against one another. Spenser's *Hymn in Honour of Love* gives one of the classic expositions of this idea:

> The earth the air the water and the fire
> Then gan to range themselves in huge array
> And with contrary forces to conspire
> Each against other by all means they may,
> Threat'ning their own confusion and decay:
> Air hated earth and water hated fire,
> Till Love relented their rebellious ire.
>
> He then them took and, tempering goodly well
> Their contrary dislikes with loved means,
> Did place them all in order and compel
> To keep themselves within their sundry reigns
> Together linkt with adamantine chains;
> Yet so that as in every living wight
> They mix themselves and show their kindly might.

Since the macrocosm is made stable by the establishment of a harmony of opposites therein, one can assume that a similar *concordia discors* is the desirable state for the microcosm, man. And so it is, according to the well-known theory of the four "humors" that make up the human constitution. These are melancholy, (cold and dry, corresponds to earth); phlegm (cold and moist, corresponds to water); blood (hot and moist, corresponds to air); and choler (hot and dry, corresponds to fire). The more evenly balanced one's humors, the better a person's health and temperament. The excessive predominance of one humor would, of course, lead to trouble: one might be excessively "choleric" and hot-tempered, for example. The last two lines of the passage from Spenser just quoted assert the analogy between the elements and the humors. The "humors" characters with which the Renaissance stage teems are the victims of humorous imbalance.

By the eighteenth century much of the Elizabethan world picture has faded. We no longer find a literal belief in a creation of specifically defined analogous planes, or a universe of potentially warring elements held together in harmonious discord by God's love. One thing that remains, however, is a general tendency to think analogically. Unlike our own, the eighteenth-century mind does not compartmentalize various areas of experience. Where we are inclined to stress differences among, say, religion and art and politics and science, our eighteenth-century predecessors are more likely to seek or be impressed by similarities among them. It is to such a habit of mind that the logical strategy of Pope's *Essay on Man* appeals. Pope proceeds from the laws of "the Universe" in Epistle 1 of the *Essay* to consideration of the mind, the state, and so on, in the subsequent epistles. And once his (eighteenth-century) reader has acquiesced in certain basic principles in Epistle 1, he's hooked: he *must* accept them as Pope moves on from metaphysics to psychology/ethics and to political theory. The principle of *concordia discors* also lingers on in an altered form. While Pope and his contemporaries may not take the "four elements" theory literally, they do show a marked tendency to organize experience in terms of sets of oppositions and to conceive of the good as a mean between extremes or tension of opposites. (Obviously the classical concept of the "golden mean" comes into the picture here as well.) As a result of the combination of "analogous" thinking with the belief in the good as balance, we find the idea of concordant discord appearing in discussions of everything from politics to poetry in the eighteenth century. Thus, we find John Dryden in *The Medal* describing the ideal government for England as a tension between the claims of individual freedom on the one hand and those of established law and custom, as embodied for him in the monarchy, on the other:

> Our temp'rate isle will no extremes sustain
> Of pop'lar sway or arbitrary reign,
> But slides between them both into the best,
> Secure in freedom, in a monarch blest

In the realm of aesthetics, discussion often tends to be organized in terms of the contrast between art characterized by adherence to the classical "rules," technical correctness, and good judgment and that distinguished by passion, originality, genius, and so on. Dryden sets up his *Essay of Dramatic Poesy* in large part in terms of a contrast between the French theater with its rigid adherence to the classical rules and the English theater of the past generation with its less polished liveliness. The ideal work of art for the neoclassicist was a blend of perspiration and inspiration. "True wit," for Pope in the *Essay on Criticism,* "is nature to advantage dressed": nature blended with but not emasculated by the devices of the conscious artist. We find a similar set of antitheses dominating discussions of ethics and psychology. Here a contrast is usually made between qualities like reason and feeling, or propriety and spontaneity. In Epistle 2 of the *Essay on Man,* dealing with the ideal moral and emotional state, Pope conducts his argument in terms of what he calls "Self-Love," the active, instinctive, appetitive part of our nature, and "Reason," the calm, restraining, deliberative part. The ideal state is, needless to say, a *concordia discors* between the two:

> Two Principles in human nature reign;
> Self-love, to urge, and Reason, to restrain;
> Nor this a good, nor that a bad we call,
> Each works its end, to move or govern all:
> And to their proper operation still,

Ascribe all Good: to their improper, Ill.
Self-love, the spring of motion, acts the soul;
Reason's comparing balance rules the whole.
Man, but for that, no action could attend,
And but for this, were active to no end.

In Henry Fielding's *Tom Jones* the moral growth of Tom is presented as the addition of "prudence and religion" to Tom's basically good nature. Tom, as we see him originally, is generous, emotionally sensitive, benevolent, but he lacks the self-restraint, the ability to calculate consequences, the worldly wisdom of his antithesis and rival, Mr. Blifil. In the course of his adventures Tom acquires a share of these latter qualities; becomes a reasonable approximation to his role model, the statically perfect, prudent, *and* benevolent Squire Allworthy; and is then eligible for all of the good things that the book has to offer. Prudence and benevolence, reason and feeling, wit and judgment, unspoiled natural beauty versus the beauty of the works of man: antitheses like these are constantly cropping up in eighteenth-century literature of all sorts. Perhaps the best general terms that can be applied to these various kinds of antitheses are the terms "art" and "nature," and it is a scholarly commonplace to say that the eighteenth-century mind tends to organize thought in terms of "art–nature" contrasts of one sort or another. It is customary also to say that as we move from one end of the century to another we can trace an increasing value for "nature" in its various forms over "art," under the influence of romanticism and "democratic" political and social thinking. With these two more or less universally acknowledged commonplaces in mind we can now return to Jane Austen and *Pride and Prejudice*.

ART AND NATURE IN *PRIDE AND PREJUDICE*

Early in the novel there is a scene where Austen contrasts the musical performance of Elizabeth and Mary Bennet at Sir William Lucas's party (25). Mary, "in consequence of being the only plain one in the family," has "worked hard for knowledge and accomplishments," and her performance is technically far superior to Elizabeth's. But Mary's performance is *mere* technical accomplishment, without feeling or grace. Elizabeth, although her playing is technically "by no means capital," plays with spirit and without pedantry and is the more popular performer of the two:

> Mary had neither genius nor taste; and though vanity had given her application, it had given her likewise a pedantic air and conceited manner, which would have injured a higher degree of excellence than she had reached. Elizabeth, easy and unaffected, had been listened to with much more pleasure, though not playing half so well; and Mary, at the end of a long concerto, was glad to purchase praise and gratitude by Scotch and Irish airs.

What we are getting in this scene is the aesthetic extension of the art–nature contrast. Mary, with her dry technical expertise, becomes the representative of "art"; Elizabeth, less correct but more "easy," is being associated with "nature" on the aesthetic level.

This is not the only occasion when Elizabeth and Mary are contrasted. When Jane Bennet comes down with a bad cold on the occasion of her visit to Miss Bingley at Netherfield, Elizabeth resolves to go to her sister. It is a three-mile walk over muddy fields and roads, but Elizabeth is indifferent, both to the impropriety of a young lady's walking so far alone and to the probable state of her appearance after such an excursion. As the subject is canvassed among the members of the Bennet family (32) Mary remarks, "I admire the activity of your benevolence . . . but every impulse of feeling should be guided by reason; and, in my opinion, exertion should always be in proportion to what is required." Here we encounter the "reason–feeling" or ethical extension of the art–nature antithesis. With Mary acting once again as a foil to her, Elizabeth becomes the advocate of heart over head, of spontaneous emotional response over deference to social propriety. For the contemporary reader both of these scenes contain clear signals that Austen is setting Elizabeth up as a symbolic figure in terms of the art–nature dialectic.

It should come as no surprise, then, to find Elizabeth an admirer of the unspoiled sublime in natural scenery. We have already seen in the previous chapter her admiration for the landscaping of Darcy's Pemberley, where nature is dressed to advantage but not offensively tampered with. Similarly, the prospect of a tour to the wild Lake District—this, we recall is the "Wordsworth" country, dear to the romantic poets and their admirers—fills Elizabeth with delight. "What are men to rocks and mountains! Oh! what hours of transport we shall spend!" (154).

Finally, and most important for our purposes, we should consider Elizabeth's democratic streak, her insistence on dealing with people as individuals, without regard to their social or economic standing. Thus, she responds to Mr. Wickham solely in terms of what he is in himself—or seems to her to be in himself—without reference to his low birth and lack of money. It takes a gentle reminder from Aunt Gardiner to make her acknowledge the social disaster that marriage to him would be and alert her to the danger of falling in love with him. Her horror at Charlotte Lucas's accepting the personally distasteful Mr. Collins for social and economic reasons has already been commented upon. Again, Elizabeth is conspicuously unimpressed by Lady Catherine de Bourgh's wealth and consequence. Austen humorously contrasts the fear and trembling with which Sir William Lucas and his daughter Maria contemplate their introduction to Lady Catherine with Elizabeth's sangfroid on the same occasion (161–62): "When they ascended the steps to the hall, Maria's alarm was every moment increasing, and even Sir William did not look perfectly calm.—Elizabeth's courage did not fail her. She had heard nothing of Lady Catherine that spoke her awful from any extraordinary talents or miraculous virtue, and the mere stateliness of money and rank, she thought she could witness without trepidation." Uninfluenced by Lady Catherine's social status—or, if influenced, influenced adversely, as the catty tone of the next observation might suggest—she finds her simply "a tall, large woman, with strongly-marked features, which might once have been handsome. Her air was not conciliating, nor was her manner of receiving them, such as to make her visitors forget their inferior rank. She was not rendered formidable by silence; but whatever she said, was spoken in so authoritative a tone, as marked her self-importance."

Elizabeth exemplifies "nature" in the realm of social relations—as in the realm of morality, in her aesthetic practice and preference, in her basic temperament.

The extent to which the art–nature contrast permeates *Pride and Prejudice* is extraordinary, and one does not begin to appreciate the structural tightness and economy that are characteristic of the novel until he has read the book in terms of the antithesis. Samuel Kliger, from whose seminal article on *Pride and Prejudice* most of the examples cited on the previous pages have been derived, holds that "The governing idea of *Pride and Prejudice* is the art–nature antithesis; the perfection of form is achieved through relating each character and incident to the basic art–nature dialectic.[6] We may note, for instance, the fact that the girls of the Bennet family are arranged along a spectrum from an extreme of "art" to an extreme of "nature." At one end of the scale is Mary, buried in books and coldly cerebral. At the other are Kitty and Lydia, empty-headed, mannerless followers of impulses and of anything that wears a uniform. In nearer to a mean, are Jane and Elizabeth. Jane errs slightly on the side of "art," I believe: her extreme reserve and self-restraint, while admirably intended, certainly do her disservice in her love affair with Bingley. Elizabeth, for her part, errs in the direction of "nature" in various ways, but can be, and is, brought closer to the mean in the course of the story. There is also a pattern involving Lady Catherine de Bourgh, Darcy, Elizabeth, and Mr. Bennet. Lady Catherine and Mr. Bennet are set up as antitheses to one another in several ways. He, as we have seen, shows witty, socially irreverent intelligence, which he has passed on to his favorite daughter, accompanied by social irresponsibility. Lady Catherine, on the other hand, demonstrates a sort of noblesse oblige run mad—dictatorially interfering or attempting to interfere right and left in the lives of those around her, inspecting the shelves in Mr. Collins's closets—and arrogant stuffiness. Lady Catherine is to Darcy as Mr. Bennet is to Elizabeth. We see her as representing an extreme form of tendencies that in Darcy can be modified and made acceptable—as what Darcy might have become under certain circumstances; Mr. Bennet is an opposite extreme that finds more wholesome expression in the Elizabeth of the conclusion of the novel. We might also note the way in which the weddings in the novel arrange themselves on a scale ranging from marriages of the head to marriages of the heart. The Charlotte Lucas–Mr. Collins marriage is, of course, purely a marriage of the head: Charlotte enters into it with feelings of, at best, tolerance for her husband. At the other extreme is Lydia Bennet's marriage, which, although "heart" may be too kind a term to apply to it, is certainly based on some portion of the anatomy rather than on any rational considerations. In between we have the marriages of Jane and Elizabeth Bennet. Both young women make socially acceptable—indeed socially advantageous—matches that are at the same time motived by deep, genuine love.[7]

It is the last and, obviously, the most impoi
riages, that of Elizabeth and Darcy, to which we
more detail. For the love plot of the novel is no
witty and articulate battle of the sexes; it is
terms of personal relationships, of a pattern of oppos
mate reconciliation between the values of "art" and "natui
comprehensive eighteenth-century senses of these terms.

Just as Mary Bennet is often used to point up Elizabeth Bennet's "naturalness," so Mr. Bingley frequently serves to establish his friend Darcy as a representative of "art." One evening during Elizabeth's stay at Netherfield there is a scene in which the two men's styles of letter writing are contrasted (47–48). Darcy is employed in editing a letter to his sister, and Miss Bingley is employed in interrupting him with flattery and unnecessary messages to Miss Darcy. After "perpetual commendations . . . on his handwriting . . . on the evenness of his lines . . . on the length of his letter," she concludes her paean by declaring, "It is a rule with me, that a person who can write a long letter with ease, cannot write ill." At this point Bingley enters the conversation:

"That will not do for a compliment to Darcy, Caroline," cried her brother—"because he does *not* write with ease. He studies too much for words of four syllables.—Do not you, Darcy?"

"My stile of writing is very different from yours."

"Oh!" cried Miss Bingley, "Charles writes in the most careless way imaginable. He leaves out half his words, and blots the rest."

"My ideas flow so rapidly that I have not time to express them—by which means my letters sometimes convey no ideas at all to my correspondents."

Darcy's epistolary style exemplifies "art" in the aesthetic extension of the art–nature antithesis. He writes slowly, at length, and with care for all the details of his performance from vocabulary to calligraphy. Bingley, on the other hand, writes "naturally," spilling out his thoughts and emotions without regard to the rules of composition or penmanship. This contrast of their epistolary performances parallels the comparison between the musical performances of Elizabeth and Mary

the conversation goes on to place Darcy in terms of another opposition, the art-nature antithesis, the reason–feeling or ethical extension lowers of judges Bingley's epistolary deficiencies as part of a between a tendency to be swayed by the impulse or emotion of the on this citing as evidence Bingley's declaration to Mrs. Bennet that regarding the rapidity with which he would act if he were to take it into his head to leave Netherfield. "You are really proud of your defects in writing," says Darcy,

"because you consider them as proceeding from a rapidity of thought and carelessness of execution, which if not estimable, you think at least highly interesting. The power of doing anything with quickness is always much prized by the possessor, and often without any attention to the imperfection of the performance. When you told Mrs. Bennet this morning that if you ever resolved on quitting Netherfield you should be gone in five minutes, you meant it to be a sort of panegyric, of compliment to yourself—and yet what is there so very laudable in a precipitance which must leave very necessary business undone, and can be of no real advantage to yourself or anyone else?"

Moreover, Darcy adds, Bingley's "precipitance" in this instance could be equally hastily counteracted by a new emotional impulse: "Your conduct would be quite as dependent on chance as that of any man I know; and if, as you were mounting your horse, a friend were to say, 'Bingley, you had better stay till next week,' you would probably do it, you would probably not go —and, at another word, might stay a month."

Not surprisingly, at this point Elizabeth leaps to Bingley's defense. Yielding to the impulse of friendship is, for her, an admirable thing, and Darcy's description of Bingley's tendency to do so has "shewn him off now much more than he did himself." Darcy attempts to defend himself in the following dialogue:

> "You must remember, Miss Bennet, that the friend who is supposed to desire his return to the house, and the delay of his plan, has merely desired it, asked it without argument in favour of its propriety."
>
> "To yield readily—easily—to the *persuasion* of a friend has no merit with you."
>
> "To yield without conviction is no compliment to the understanding of either."
>
> "You appear to me, Mr. Darcy, to allow nothing for the influence of friendship and affection. A regard for the requester would often make one readily yield to a request, without waiting for arguments to reason one into it."

Darcy, then, is playing "reason" to Bingley's and Elizabeth's "feeling," calm calculation of consequences to their advocacy of impulse-based behavior. Thus it is scarcely surprising that Elizabeth's "precipitance" in walking to Netherfield should receive scant support from him when it comes under attack from Miss Bingley and Mrs. Hurst (35–36). To Bingley the action shows "an affection for her sister that is very pleasing." But when Miss Bingley asks Darcy whether he would wish to see his sister "make such an exhibition," his reply is a firm, "certainly not."

Most important, Darcy reverses the tendency we have seen in Elizabeth to deal with people "naturally" (i.e., without regard for their places in the social context). He is very conscious of, and a strong advocate of, class distinctions. The balls of the Meryton neighborhood, delightful to the gregarious Bingley, are distasteful to him because of the mixed bag of social types they bring together on a temporarily equal footing. He is offended when Mr. Collins attempts to converse with him without an introduction. Miss Bingley's and Mrs. Hurst's remarks about the Bennet girls' "uncle near Cheapside" draw indignation from the democratic Bingley, who considers Jane and Elizabeth for what they are in themselves. "If they had uncles enough to fill *all* Cheapside," he cries, "it would not make them one jot less agreeable" (37). But Darcy answers that "it must very materially lessen their chances of marrying men of any consideration in the world." Again, it is Darcy's class pride that is in large part responsible for his conceited assumptions regarding his matrimonial desirability in Elizabeth's eyes. And the sense of class distinctions surfaces at its most blatant and unattractive in his first proposal (189–92): "His sense of her inferiority—of its being a degradation—of the family obstacles which judgment had always opposed to inclination, were dwelt on with a warmth which seemed due to the consequence he was wounding, but was very unlikely to recommend his suit." At the angry conclusion of the scene he asks: "Could you expect me to rejoice in the inferiority of your connections? To congratulate myself on the hope of relations . . . so decidedly beneath my own?"

What is at the bottom of the antagonism that separates Darcy and Elizabeth, then, is the clash between "art" and "nature" in their comprehensive eighteenth-century meanings. The "tendencies to particular evils," the causes of the moral blindness dealt with in the previous chapter, are tendencies classifiable in the terminology of the art–nature dialectic. Elizabeth is initially an extreme of "nature," quick intelligence, strong feelings, spontaneity, a regard for people as individuals, indifference to or distrust of rank and wealth. Darcy, nearer the opposite end of the scale, is slower moving, cautious, rational, attentive to considerations of propriety, and much alive to class distinctions. Their growth toward self-knowledge and one another is growth away from extremes toward a mean. Darcy sees the attractions of Elizabeth's "nature" and through his experiences with her modifies his class pride. Elizabeth sees the worth of Darcy's solid qualities and acknowledges the positive side of class orientation. Neither reverses his ideas or temperament completely, of course. Their marriage will be a *concordia discors* in which each balances and modifies qualities in the other to advantage. Elizabeth, we are told, envisioned just such an interaction when all hope of Darcy seemed lost:

> She began now to comprehend that he was exactly the man, who in disposition and talents, would most suit her. His understanding and temper, though unlike her own, would have answered all her wishes. It was a union that must have been to the advantage of both; by her ease and liveliness, his mind might have been softened, his manners improved, and from his judgment, information, and knowledge of the world, she must have received benefit of greater importance. (312)

Fortunately for both, hope was not lost.

The art–nature dialectic, in various forms, underlies all of Austen's other novels, as well as *Pride and Prejudice*. In *Northanger Abbey* the "natural" Catherine Morland, fresh from a country rectory, takes on the complex social world of Bath and comes to terms with it. In *Mansfield Park* a relationship is worked out between the gauche but morally upright and sensitive Fanny Price and her relatives, the wealthy and worldly Bertram family. In *Emma*, Emma Woodhouse plays "imagination" to the "judgment" of the hero, Mr. Knightley. *Persuasion* places the heroine Anne Elliot between her cautious and rather snobbish mother-surrogate, Lady Russell, and Anne's lover, the bold and democratic Captain Wentworth. The title of *Sense and Sensibility* speaks for itself. And reading the novels in terms of the art–nature contrast enables us to see the extent to which Austen is in touch with the larger intellectual and social currents of her generation. The popular nineteenth- and early twentieth-century image of her—the image of a gentlewoman who, in the era that saw the revolutions of America and France, the triumph of romanticism, important economic and social change within England, confined her writing to the lives of characters who are untouched by such things and largely unaware of them—is drastically altered. If we view *Pride and Prejudice* in the light of the art–nature antithesis and bear in mind the widespread use of this dialectic in political, aesthetic, and other sorts of intellectual discourse of the period, it becomes clear that Austen is dealing, in human terms, with the forces *behind* the revolutions of her day. The differences between Elizabeth and Darcy are the differences between Paine and Burke, between romantic and classic. Their reconciliation is a philosophical stance as well as the culmination of an intricate study in personal relationships. Indeed, can one not argue that Austen's refusal to connect her work more overtly with the specific happenings of her day *adds* to its intellectual depth? Austen, I believe, sees the revolutions of her day as manifestations of forces that are universal and eternal in the human spirit. There will always be in mankind conflicts between the impulses toward order and energy, calm and warmth; between reverence for the status quo and impatience with it; between upper and lower. In a proper reading of *Pride and Prejudice* we not only see Elizabeth and Darcy as manifestations of the social, aesthetic, and other forces of their day, but also these forces as manifested in Elizabeth and Darcy (i.e., in mankind, in ourselves). *Pride and Prejudice* is not "dated," as are, say, *Uncle Tom's Cabin* or *Hard Times,* both tied to specific social issues; it is a novel for all time; it is classic. Samuel Johnson, among the eighteenth century's greatest men of letters, was one of Austen's favorite writers, perhaps her very favorite. In chapter 10 of his *Rasselas* Johnson says of the true artist that he "must divest himself of the prejudices of his age or country; he must consider right and wrong in their abstracted and invariable state; he must disregard present laws and opinions, and rise to general and transcendental truths, which will always be the same . . . He must write as . . . a being superior to time and place."

I think Jane Austen took this definition seriously.

7

SYMBOLIC MOTIFS AND "CONVERSATION SCENES" ─────

> Of all great writers she is the most difficult to catch in the act of greatness.
>
> Virginia Woolf on Jane Austen

It may be appropriate to open this chapter with a few words on the subject of Jane Austen and symbolism in general. She does not, in her earlier works at any rate, rely on "large," conspicuous symbols to embody and reflect her intellectual and emotional concerns. There is nothing in *Pride and Prejudice* that corresponds to the white whale in Melville's *Moby-Dick,* the image of Satis House in Dickens's *Great Expectations,* the Marabar Caves in Forster's *Passage to India,* or the images of the spire and the apple tree in Golding's *The Spire.* Austen does, however, employ several more modest symbolic devices with great success. She will often use certain kinds of low-keyed symbolic motifs—recurring references to an object, or a kind of object, or to a particular activity—as means for establishing and comparing characters in relation to the novel's larger thematic patterns. She also likes to stage scenes where various characters converse on a common theme or topic, and to use these scenes in a similar symbolic fashion.

Symbolic Motifs and "Conversation Scenes"

Consider, for example, how many times books, libraries, and the activity of reading are mentioned in *Pride and Prejudice,* and how much these references manage to tell us about characters and their relations to the novel's intellectual scheme. When Elizabeth is visiting at Netherfield, we learn something about the nature of Mr. Bingley's library. Elizabeth one evening decides not to join in a card game in progress after dinner and looks about for a book to read (37–38). Bingley, with his usual effusive good nature, offers "to fetch her others; all that his library afforded," and he apologizes for the small size of his rather carelessly kept-up collection: "I wish my collection were larger for your benefit and my own credit; but I am an idle fellow, and though I have not many, I have more than I ever look into." This gives Miss Bingley an opportunity to praise the size and comprehensiveness of Mr. Darcy's library at Pemberley:

> "I am astonished," said Miss Bingley, "that my father should have left so small a collection of books.—What a delightful library you have at Pemberley, Mr. Darcy."
>
> "It ought to be good," he replied, "it has been the work of many generations."
>
> "And then you have added so much to it yourself, you are always buying books."
>
> "I cannot comprehend the neglect of a family library in such days as these."

Thus the image of the library becomes an expression of the essential difference between the two men. (As well as telling us some things about Miss Bingley.) Bingley's "natural" casualness is reflected in the state of his library; Darcy's more methodical nature and his strong sense of family tradition and responsibility are shown in the excellence of his collection and in his remarks about it. The "library" motif also suggests to us some things about Mr. Bennet in contrast to Darcy. Mr. Bennet, like Darcy, had a well-stocked library. But while Darcy's is in part a sign of his acceptance of familial-social responsibility, Mr. Bennet's library is a means of escape from responsibilities. He retreats to it to avoid his obvious duty to attempt to instill a little sense into his wife and younger daughters and isolates himself in it to ignore better the results of his financial and disciplinary irresponsibility. Thus the contrast I note in chapter 5 between Darcy's sometimes stuffy but in many ways admirable orientation toward social privilege and responsibility and Mr. Bennet's sometimes amusing but ultimately culpable detachment is reinforced.

Why and how and what characters read are also symbolically suggestive. Elizabeth reads extensively because she genuinely enjoys it: an interest in intellectual exercise is part of the general, "natural" liveliness of her mind. Mary Bennet's continual, narrow immersion in "great books" from which she is "making extracts" is an indication of the pedantry that marks her leaning toward the "artificial" in the novel's "art-nature" contrast. An amusing scene at Netherfield reveals the extent to which "art" of another sort from Mary's motivates the reading of the library-loving Miss Bingley. After Darcy (who enjoys reading as Elizabeth does—an early indication of their basic compatibility) has taken up a book one evening, Miss Bingley does the same. But

> Miss Bingley's attention was quite as much engaged in watching Mr. Darcy's progress through *his* book, as in reading her own; and she was perpetually either making some inquiry, or looking at his page. She could not win him, however, to any conversation; he merely answered her question, and read on. At length, quite exhausted by the attempt to be amused with her own book, which she had only chosen because it was the second volume of his, she gave a great yawn and said, "how pleasant it is to spend an evening in this way! I believe after all there is no enjoyment like reading! How much sooner one tires of any thing than of a book!—When I have a house of my own, I shall be miserable if I have not an excellent library."
>
> No one made any reply. She then yawned again, threw aside her book, and cast her eyes round the room in quest of some amusement. (55)

Mr. Collins, spending a morning in the library at Longbourn with Mr. Bennet, is "nominally engaged with one of the largest folios in the collection, but really talking to Mr. Bennet, with little cessation, of his house and garden at Hunsford" (71). When invited to read aloud to the ladies at Longbourn, he recoils in horror from the novel they are currently reading and chooses Fordyce's *Sermons* instead, demonstrating his own stuffiness and allowing Lydia to display her empty head and bad manners by interrupting him with local gossip before he has, "with very monotonous solemnity, read three pages" (69).

Music is another important motif in *Pride and Prejudice*. As we have seen earlier, it serves, in the scene in which Mary and Elizabeth Bennet's performances are contrasted, to help place the two young women in terms of the novel's art–nature antithesis. It also acts as a basis for comparisons of a similar sort between Elizabeth and Miss Bingley. Elizabeth plays primarily because she enjoys music for its own sake, without too much regard to an audience, if there be any. For Miss Bingley, however, musical performance is one of the stock of feminine "accomplishments" that are a social status symbol and a means of attracting eligible men:

> "No one can be really esteemed accomplished, who does not greatly surpass what is usually met with. A woman must have a thorough knowledge of music, singing, drawing, dancing, and the modern languages, to deserve the word; and besides all this, she must possess a certain something in her air and manner of walking, the tone of her voice, her address and expressions, or the word will be but half deserved." (39)

She attempts to use commentary on Georgiana Darcy's progress on the harp as a means of establishing rapport between herself and Darcy (48). She is eager to display her own expertise at the piano-forte for his benefit (51), and she suggests a musical performance in order to break up a tête-à-tête between Elizabeth and Darcy that she finds threatening to her interests (58).

The "music" motif also does its delightful part in establishing Lady Catherine de Bourgh in the novel's scheme of values. When, at

Rosings, Elizabeth and Colonel Fitzwilliam are having an animated conversation about "new books and music," Lady Catherine stakes out her claim to musical taste as follows: "[Music] is of all subjects my delight. I must have my share in the conversation, if you are speaking of music. There are few people in England, I suppose, who have more true enjoyment of music than myself, or a better natural taste. If I had ever learnt, I should have been a great proficient" (173). The secret of musical excellence, following the gospel according to Lady Catherine, is, of course, unremitting technical exercise; and this she urges constantly upon Elizabeth, even offering her the use of one of the instruments at Rosings—the one in the governess's quarters:

> "I often tell young ladies that no excellence in music is to be acquired, without constant practice. I have told Miss Bennet several times, that she will never play really well, unless she practices more; and though Mrs. Collins has no instrument, she is very welcome, as I have often told her, to come to Rosings every day, and play on the pianoforte in Mrs. Jenkinson's room. She would be in nobody's way, you know, in that part of the house." (173)

Then, when Elizabeth performs for Colonel Fitzwilliam, Lady Catherine, as we have observed in an earlier chapter, listens to "half a song" and returns to her conversation with Darcy.

Natural beauty, landscaping, and characters' reactions to these things also take on a sort of symbolic function in the novel. Elizabeth is a great admirer of natural beauty. "Solitary rambles" in the wooded areas at Rosings are among her greatest pleasures during her stay with Mr. and Mrs. Collins (82). As we have seen earlier, she is delighted with the prospect of a northern excursion with the Gardiners, the principal object of which will be visiting spots of natural beauty; and she prides herself on the keenness and accuracy of her observation.

> "Oh! What hours of transport we shall spend! And when we *do* return, it shall not be like other travellers, without being able to give one accurate idea of any thing. We *will* know where we have

gone—we *will* recollect what we have seen. Lakes, mountains, and rivers, shall not be jumbled together in our imaginations; nor, when we attempt to describe any particular scene, will we begin quarrelling about its relative situation. Let *our* first effusions be less insupportable than those of the generality of travellers." (154)

The excellent landscaping of Pemberley is of symbolic significance in defining Darcy's character. Elizabeth, we remember, is much pleased by its "naturalness"; and this preference for the natural in landscaping on Darcy's part is an indication of the fact that he is not at such an extreme of the novel's "art-nature" scale as to be incapable of reaching something like the mean that the novel finds desirable. Their similar taste in landscaping, like their fondness for reading, is evidence of Elizabeth's and Darcy's being closer in spirit than she is at first willing to admit; and the perception of Pemberley's beauty, as we have seen, marks an important stage in Elizabeth's progress toward knowledge of Darcy and of herself.

Character's attitudes toward dancing and their behavior in the ballroom may also be important thematically. At one extreme, there is the Darcy of the early part of the book. His advertisement of his distaste for dancing—he stands "in silent indignation at such a mode of passing the evening, to the exclusion of all conversation" at Sir William Lucas's impromptu dance, and he replies "every savage can dance" in answer to Sir William's encomium on the pastime—marks his intellectual superciliousness. His refusal to dance with those whom he considers his social inferiors (including Elizabeth) at the Meryton assembly establishes his "improper" pride at his first appearance in the novel. On the other hand, the excessive enthusiasm of Kitty and Lydia Bennet for dancing is an outward and visible sign of their shallowness of mind: they are not capable of more intellectually demanding forms of amusement. Elizabeth, who is capable both of "teazing Colonel Forster to give us a ball" *and* of making stimulating conversation, is a desirable mean between the two extremes. Miss Bingley displays her customary eagerness to attune herself to what she supposes to be Darcy's wavelength by opposing the plans of her gregarious brother (who loves to dance) for a ball at Netherfield, providing Bingley with one of his best lines:

> "By the bye, Charles, are you really serious in meditating a dance at Netherfield?—I would advise you, before you determine on it, to consult the wishes of the present party; I am much mistaken if there are not some among us to whom a ball would be rather a punishment than a pleasure . . . I should like balls infinitely better . . . if they were carried on in a different manner; but there is something insufferably tedious in the usual process of such a meeting. It would surely be much more rational if conversation instead of dancing were made the order of the day."
>
> "Much more rational, my dear Caroline, I dare say but it would not be near so much like a ball." (55–56)

Austen even manages to make an activity as inconspicuous as walking work for her symbolically. Elizabeth is continually associated with walking: she trudges through the muddy fields to Netherfield to visit Jane; she enjoys solitary rambles at Rosings; and the scenic northern tour she so looks forward to necessarily involves a good deal of walking about. Her walking helps to establish her position in the novel's art–nature antithesis on several levels. The walk to Netherfield, as we have seen, places her in terms of the reason–feeling extension of the antithesis: she follows her heart in defiance of the rules of social convention. On another level, we note that Elizabeth's walking is associated with physically "natural" settings: with fields, with woods, with the unspoiled beauties of the North country. In contrast, there are two occasions when walking is mentioned in connection with Miss Bingley, Elizabeth's rival for Darcy's affections. She walks on the most conspicuous occasion, *in the drawing room* at Netherfield in order to draw attention to her elegant figure and carriage—and even sinks so low as to invite Elizabeth to join her when her own efforts have failed to attract Darcy's attention:

> Miss Bingley . . . got up and walked about the room. Her figure was elegant, and she walked well;—but Darcy, at whom it was all

aimed, was still inflexibly studious. In the desperation of her feelings she resolved on one effort more; and, turning to Elizabeth, said, "Miss Eliza Bennet, let me persuade you to follow my example, and take a turn about the room.—I assure you it is very refreshing after sitting so long in one attitude."

Elizabeth was surprised, but agreed to it immediately. Miss Bingley succeeded no less in the real object of her civility; Mr. Darcy looked up. (56)

The other time we see Miss Bingley walking is in the shrubbery—the most "artificial" part of the grounds—at Netherfield, on the arm of Mr. Darcy; and when Elizabeth appears on the scene with Mrs. Hurst, Elizabeth is quickly maneuvered into a position where she cannot accompany the other three (53–54). (Parenthetically, is it perhaps suggestive that Darcy's and Elizabeth's final understanding of one another is reached, and his second proposal made, in the course of a country walk, while the first, angry, proposal scene occurs in a sitting room?)

In addition to employing the motifs just discussed, Austen also uses "conversation scenes" in which several characters make contrasting comments on a common topic, to emphasize characters' thematic roles. One notable example of this technique is the conversation on Darcy's pride that occurs at the end of Vol. 1, chapter 5. Some members of the Lucas family have called on the Bennets on the morning after the Meryton assembly at which Darcy has declined to dance with Elizabeth. Mrs. Bennet begins the discussion of pride by describing Darcy as

"ate up with pride . . . Another time, Lizzy . . . I would not dance with *him*, if I were you."

"I believe, Ma'am, I may safely promise you *never* to dance with him."

"His pride," said Miss Lucas, "does not offend *me* so much as pride often does, because there is an excuse for it. One cannot wonder that so very fine a young man, with family, fortune, every thing in his favour, should think highly of himself. If I may so express it, he has a *right* to be proud."

"That is very true," replied Elizabeth, "and I could easily forgive *his* pride, if he had not mortified *mine*."

"Pride," observed Mary, who piqued herself upon the solidity of her reflections, "is a very common failing I believe. By all that I have ever read, I am convinced that it is very common indeed, that human nature is particularly prone to it, and that there are very few of us who do not cherish a feeling of self-complacency on the score of some quality or other, real or imaginary. Vanity and pride are different things, though the words are often used synonimously. A person may be proud without being vain. Pride relates more to our opinion of ourselves, vanity to what we would have others think of us." (19–20)

(The talk then degenerates into an argument between Mrs. Bennet and a "young Lucas" who declares that, had he Mr. Darcy's money, he would keep hounds and "drink a bottle of wine every day.") In this scene Mrs. Bennet reveals her inanity, as usual. Charlotte Lucas's preoccupation with economics and social standing is emphasized by her partial defense of Darcy on the grounds of his rank and wealth. Elizabeth's quickness of mind is demonstrated in her brisk, witty remarks. And Mary's ponderous pedantry helps to establish her position as an extreme of "art" and foil to Elizabeth in the novel's art–nature contrast. In the case of Mary and Elizabeth, moreover, contrasting commentary is heightened by an undercurrent of literary allusion, a topic to be discussed at length later in this study. Here both young women are echoing passages from Adam Smith's *Theory of Moral Sentiments* (1759), an extremely popular work of the day and one that Austen would expect her audience to be familiar with. In part 6, section 3, of the *Theory of Moral Sentiments* Smith is concerned with what he calls the "principle of self-estimation," which can manifest itself in vanity or pride or both. According to Smith, when proud or vain men "assume upon us, or set themselves before us, their self-estimation mortifies our own. Our own pride and vanity prompt us to accuse them of pride and vanity, and we cease to be the impartial spectators of their conduct."[8]

Symbolic Motifs and "Conversation Scenes"

Elizabeth, with her light and lively mind, has appropriated Smith's idea and made it her own when she remarks that Darcy's pride has "mortified her own." Mary's ponderous and uncalled-for distinction between pride and vanity, however, is lifted almost verbatim from Smith. Smith states that

> our dislike to pride and vanity generally disposes us to rank the persons whom we accuse of these vices rather below than above the common level . . . I think we are most frequently in the wrong, and that both the proud man and the vain man are often (perhaps for the most part) a good deal above it; though not near so much as the one really thinks himself, or as the other wishes you to think him. (378)

He further remarks that

> the proud man is often vain; and the vain man is often proud. Nothing can be more natural than that the man who thinks much more highly of himself than he deserves should wish that other people should think still more highly of him; or that the man who wishes that other people should think more highly of him than he thinks of himself should, at the same time, think much more highly of himself than he deserves. (380)

Clearly the *Theory of Moral Sentiments* is one of those "great books" from which Mary extracts her reflections, and her inappropriate near-plagiarism reinforces our sense of her pedantry. The contrast between the two young women's styles of "borrowing" from the same work emphasizes the larger kinds of contrasts between them.

A similar scene occurs when the Bennet family receives the letter in which Mr. Collins invites himself to Longbourn for a visit, hinting at possible "amends" to the family for the entail of the estate and hoping, in a cliché that would have been even more conspicuous to Austen's contemporaries than it is to us, that Mr. Bennet will not "reject the offered olive branch." (The section of this study on literary allusion will explain the special quality of this metaphor for Austen's contemporaries.) Mr. Bennet, having read the letter aloud remarks

"At four o'clock, therefore, we may expect this peace-making gentleman," . . . He seems to be a most conscientious and polite young man, upon my word; and I doubt not will prove a valuable acquaintance, especially if Lady Catherine should be so indulgent as to let him come to us again."

[Mrs. Bennet:] "There is some sense in what he says about the girls, however; and if he is disposed to make them any amends, I shall not be the person to discourage him."

"Though it is difficult," said Jane, "to guess in what way he can mean to make us the atonement he thinks our due, the wish is certainly to his credit."

Elizabeth was chiefly struck with his extraordinary deference for Lady Catherine, and his kind intention of christening, marrying and burying his parishioners whenever it were required.

"He must be an oddity, I think," said she. "I cannot make him out.—There is something very pompous in his stile.—And what can he mean by apologizing for being next in the entail?—We cannot suppose he would help it, if he could.—Can he be a sensible man, sir?"

"No, my dear, I think not. I have great hopes of finding him quite the reverse. There is a mixture of servility and self-importance in his letter, which promises well. I am impatient to see him."

"In point of composition," said Mary, "his letter does not seem defective. The idea of the olive branch perhaps is not wholly new, yet I think it is well expressed."

To Catherine and Lydia, neither the letter nor its writer were in any degree interesting. It was next to impossible that their cousin should come in a scarlet coat, and it was now some weeks since they had received pleasure from the society of a man in any other colour. (64–65).

Mr. Bennet's detached, cynical enjoyment of folly and pomposity and Elizabeth's shrewd and amused perception of them are typically displayed in their remarks. Mrs. Bennet reveals the mercenary turn of her mind; Jane, the somewhat saccharine "candour" (i.e., in eighteenth-century phraseology, disposition to think well of people in general) characteristic of her. Mary, true to form, is concerned with the technical aspects of the letter's composition and picks out its most resounding cliché for special praise. And Kitty and Lydia's "minds" are revealed as well.

The scene referred to earlier in which Bingley's and Darcy's libraries are compared is part of a larger conversation on books and reading in general that begins when Elizabeth has declined to play cards. Mr. Hurst looks at her "with astonishment":

> "Do you prefer reading to cards?" said he; "that is rather singular."
>
> "Miss Eliza Bennet," said Miss Bingley, "despises cards. She is a great reader, and has no pleasure in any thing else."
>
> "I deserve neither such praise nor such censure," cried Elizabeth; "I am *not* a great reader, and I have pleasure in many things."
>
> "In nursing your sister I am sure you have pleasure," said Bingley; "and I will hope it will soon be increased by seeing her quite well." (37)

(Elizabeth then begins to choose a book, and Bingley's offers, apologies, and the comparison of libraries follow.) Thus, before our attention is focused on the contrast between Darcy and Bingley as revealed by their libraries, we have also observed Mr. Hurst's intellectual vacuity, Miss Bingley's bitchy sexual tactics, Elizabeth's quickness to respond in characteristically energetic and incisive phrasing, and Bingley's good-natured anxiety to smooth out the sharper edges of conversation and life.

Similar "conversation" scenes occur with frequency throughout *Pride and Prejudice*. One might cite, for instance, the varied responses elicited by Elizabeth's wish to walk to Netherfield and see Jane (31–32), already mentioned in another context in chapter 6, or the scene where members of the Bennet family and Mr. Collins react to the invitation to Mr. Bingley's ball at Netherfield (86–87). Such scenes seem to me to occur with more frequency in *Pride and Prejudice* than in any other of Austen's novels. They remain, however, an important part of her literary stock-in-trade throughout her career.

All of the things dealt with in this chapter concern material drawn from the ordinary, everyday lives of the more-or-less typical gentlefolk with whom Austen chooses to deal. Very little "happens" in the way of dramatic or extraordinary action in an Austen novel: characters visit and converse, take walks, play and sing a bit, attend the occasional ball or party (the most "dramatic" incident in the novel—Lydia's elopement—resolves itself into a less-than-desirable marriage). Yet Austen is able to "get" so much from this seemingly rather commonplace material. With an economy that is perhaps her strongest claim to greatness, she can make the choice of a book, the style of a musical performance, a seemingly casual conversation do thematic work that, in another sort of novelist, might occupy pages of exposition. (Trollope, in the Barset novels, would be an appropriate contrast, given the analogous social milieu.) An appreciation of Austen's work must be in part an appreciation of low-keyed economy, of effects achieved by detail and proportion, of suggestive understatement: "Of all great writers she is the most difficult to catch in the act of greatness." The Victorian exuberance and color and (sometimes rather shapeless) variety of a Charles Dickens is not there. But is the Victorian bouquet, where everything in the garden is jammed in in many-hued profusion, necessarily superior to the classical Japanese flower arrangement where minimal materials—and the spaces between them—make another kind of beauty?

8

VERBAL STYLES

Some Prefatory Remarks:
The Mind's Eye and the Mind's Ear

This is the beginning of George Eliot's *Adam Bede*:

> With a single drop of ink for a mirror, the Egyptian sorcerer
> undertakes to reveal to any chance comer far-reaching visions of the
> past. This is what I undertake to do for you, reader. With this drop
> of ink at the end of my pen, I will show you the roomy workshop
> of Mr. Jonathan Burge, carpenter and builder, in the village of
> Hayslope, as it appeared on the eighteenth of June, in the year of
> our Lord 1799.
>
> The afternoon sun was warm on the five workmen there, busy
> upon doors and window-frames and wainscoting. A scent of pine-
> wood from a tentlike pile of planks outside the open door mingled
> itself with the scent of the elder-bushes which were spreading their
> summer snow close to the open window opposite; the slanting sun-
> beams shone through the transparent shavings that flew before the
> steady plane, and lit up the fine grain of the oak panelling which
> stood propped against the wall.
>
> On a heap of those soft shavings a rough, grey shepherd dog
> had made himself a pleasant bed, and was lying with his nose be-
> tween his forepaws, occasionally wrinkling his brows to cast a
> glance at the tallest of the five workmen, who was carving a shield
> in the centre of a wooden mantelpiece. . . . [Adam Bede] showed an

arm that was likely to win the prize for feats of strength; yet the long supple hand, with its broad finger-tips, looked ready for works of skill. In his tall stalwartness Adam Bede was a Saxon, and justified his name; but the jet-black hair, made the more noticeable by its contrast with the light paper cap, and the keen glance of the dark eyes that shone from under strongly marked, prominent and mobile eyebrows, indicated a mixture of Celtic blood.

Here is the opening of *Pride and Prejudice:*

It is a truth universally acknowledged, that a single man in possession of a good fortune must be in want of a wife.

However little known the feelings or views of such a man may be on his first entering a neighborhood, this truth is so well fixed in the minds of the surrounding families, that he is considered as the rightful property of some one or other of their daughters.

"My dear Mr. Bennet," said his lady to him one day, "have you heard that Netherfield Park is let at last?"

Mr. Bennet replied that he had not.

"But it is," returned she; "for Mrs. Long has just been there, and she told me all about it."

Mr. Bennet made no answer.

"Do you not want to know who has taken it?" cried his wife impatiently.

"*You* want to tell me, and I have no objection to hearing it."

This was invitation enough.

"Why, my dear, you must know, Mrs. Long says that Netherfield is taken by a young man of large fortune from the north of England; that he came down on Monday in a chaise and four to see the place, and was so much delighted with it that he agreed with Mr. Morris immediately, and some of his servants are to be in the house by the end of next week."

When one compares the two passages what is most immediately apparent is that while George Eliot is relying very heavily on visual impressions for her effects, Jane Austen makes practically no appeal to them at all. The passage from *Adam Bede* gives us a very specific setting. There are five workmen and a dog in a carpenters' shop that is lit by warm afternoon sun and filled with pieces of panelling and heaps of shavings. Individual components of the scene are described in detail: Adam is not merely carving, but carving a shield in the center of a mantlepiece. He himself is tall, stalwart, with large biceps, rough-hewn features, thick eyebrows. There is much emphasis on color and texture: Adam has jet-black hair; his dog is a rough, gray shepherd-dog; sunbeams shine through transparent shavings and light up fine-grained oak. In the passage from *Pride and Prejudice* there *is* no particular setting. The scene could be taking place in Mr. Bennet's study, in the morning room, the drawing room—no location is specified. There are no details of furnishing or decor, here or elsewhere in the chapter. We know almost nothing about Mr. and Mrs. Bennet's physical characteristics—indeed, in the entire first chapter we learn only that Mrs. Bennet is "handsome" in some fashion not specified. What Austen is relying upon to "carry" the scene for us is the dialogue between the Bennets. We can "hear" their individual voices so vividly that we are drawn into their world and engaged by it. The entire first chapter of *Pride and Prejudice,* in fact, consists of three brief paragraphs of authorial comment, two at the beginning and one at the end, and some thirty-odd speeches by Mr. and Mrs. Bennet. There is not a single word referring to appearance other than the adjective "handsome," applied first to Mrs. Bennet and later to her daughter Lydia, and the equally abstract term "beauty," applied to Mrs. Bennet.

The opening of *Pride and Prejudice* is representative of the rest of the book. There is almost no visual dimension to this novel (or to any other of Austen's works, for that matter). What color is Elizabeth Bennet's hair? What was she wearing on the night when Darcy refused to dance with her—or on any other occasion in the book, one might add? What do we know of Darcy's appearance other than the fact that he is "tall" and "handsome"? What do the drawing rooms at Longbourn or Netherfield look like? Austen is little interested in appealing to the mind's eye. It is to the "mind's ear," as it were, that she appeals, relying, with extraordinary success, on aural effects to bring her work to life. Each character in *Pride and Prejudice*—and the narrator as well—has a distinctive verbal style. And the manipulation of verbal styles serves not only to vivify characters and create brilliant scenes but also to place characters in terms of the novel's themes. Before examining some particular styles and their functions it is useful to consider two reasons, one negative, the other positive, for Austen's preference for aural over visual effects.

What probably leads her to play down the visual is her inheritance from neoclassical aesthetics. Minute visual detail was frowned upon by traditional neoclassical critical theory. The artist, according to critics such as Samuel Johnson and Sir Joshua Reynolds, sees and renders the general and universal aspects of the particular material with which he is dealing. Too much specificity of detail may interfere with this. The famous "streaks of the tulip" passage from chapter 10 of Johnson's *Rasselas* is the classic illustration of this position:

> The business of a poet . . . is to examine, not the individual, but the species; to remark general properties and large appearances: he does not number the streaks of the tulip, or describe the different shades in the verdure of the forest. He is to exhibit in his portraits of nature such prominent and striking features, as recall the original to every mind; and must neglect the minuter discriminations, which one may have remarked, and another have neglected, for those characteristicks which are alike obvious to vigilance and carelessness.

The relatively abstract quality of much of neoclassical poetry is the result of this aesthetic. Even in a "descriptive" poem like Pope's *Windsor Forest* we find that general features of the landscape, rather than distinctive particulars, are stressed:

> Here hills and vales, the woodland and the plain,
> Here earth and water seem to strive again;
> Not chaos-like, together crushed and bruised,
> But, as the world, harmoniously confused:
> Where order in variety we see,
> And where, though all things differ, all agree.
> Here waving groves a chequered scene display,
> And part admit, and part exclude the day;
> As some coy nymph, her lover's warm address
> Nor quite indulges, nor can quite repress.
> There, interspersed in lawns and opening glades,

Thin trees arise that shun each other's shades.
Here in full light the russet plains extend:
There wrapped in clouds the bluish hills ascend.

"Color" words are comparatively few—"russet," "bluish"—and the emphasis is less on the landscape per se than on the manner in which it exemplifies the ideal of "order in variety," of *concordia discors*, that underlies the poem.

That Austen approved of the neoclassical principle of nonparticularity is evident in a piece of advice she gave to an aspiring fellow novelist, her niece Anna Austen. Anna sent sections of a manuscript on which she was working to her aunt for criticism, and in a letter of 9 September 1814 Jane Austen advises: "You describe a sweet place, but your descriptions are often more minute than will be liked. You give too many particulars of right hand and left" (*Letters*, 401). The comparative absence of visual detail in her own work is the result of her putting her neoclassical precepts into practice.

To understand Austen's preference for, and heavy reliance upon, aural effects, one must be able to relate to a concept of "reading" that is very different from the one to which we, as twentieth-century readers, are accustomed. One cannot emphasize too strongly the fact that all eighteenth- and early nineteenth-century literature is to a large extent designed for reading aloud. Literature is still in part an oral-aural medium in Austen's day. We should probably do best to think of a novel of the period as something between our idea of a novel—something that goes from printed page to eye to mind—and a dramatic recitation, or perhaps a radio show, in which matter goes from voice to ear to mind. (It should be interesting to see what effect the increasing trend of reproducing novels on cassette tapes has on the appreciation of Austen.) Reading aloud was one of the most common forms of recreation among the literate classes of Austen's time. Even in Mrs. Bennet's far from intellectual family circle, we remember, the women are in the habit of reading to one another of an evening. There is a novel in progress, which he rejects in favor of Fordyce's sermons, when Mr. Collins is invited to perform for them. Novels of the period, then, were written not only with an eye to the solitary reader but with an "ear" to the listener. Moreover, given the universal attunement to reading aloud, authors could expect a high degree of imaginative aural sensitivity even from the solitary reader.

The Austens' family circle, even more than most, were great readers aloud. In what survives of Austen's much-mutilated correspondence there are six references to the practice. In one, of particular interest for our purposes, she complains that her mother is not performing well in a reading of *Pride and Prejudice* itself. Writing to her sister Cassandra, who is away on a visit, Jane says, "Our second reading to Miss Benn had not pleased me so well, but I believe something must be attributed to my mother's too rapid way getting on: and though she perfectly understands the characters herself, she cannot speak as they ought" (*Letters*, 299). The Austens were a highly literate family, and several Austens tried their hands at creative writing. Apparently many of their endeavors were either produced for, or tried out upon, one another in oral performance. Austen honed her own skills in large part by the reading-aloud process. Her juvenilia—*Love and Freindship*, and the recently discovered *Sir Charles Grandison*, for example—are obviously designed for the entertainment of the family circle, as all sorts of internal evidence make clear. And her sister Cassandra, especially, was a respected critic to whom her work was read throughout Jane's life. We have then in Austen a writer whose cultural background would lead her to regard her art as in a high degree an oral-aural one, and whose particular family circumstances would heighten this tendency considerably. No wonder that verbal styles assume such importance in her work and that she learns to handle them with consummate skill.

VERBAL STYLES IN *PRIDE AND PREJUDICE*: THE NARRATIVE VOICE

We must begin with Austen's own verbal style as narrator, for the narrative voice of *Pride and Prejudice* provides the norms against which characters' individual voices emerge by comparison and, rather more often, contrast.[9]

As far as vocabulary is concerned, perhaps the most notable feature is the frequent use of abstract, often conceptual, terms and a correspondingly small reliance on heavily concrete terminology. Norman Page, in one of the best studies of Austen's style, remarks upon "the conspicuous absence of words referring to physical perceptions, the world of . . . sensuous response; and on the other hand, the recurrence of . . . words . . . mainly epithets and abstract nouns indicating personal qualities—qualities, that is, of character and temperament rather than of outward appearance."[10]

The description of Mr. and Mrs. Bennet at the conclusion of chapter 1 illustrates this quality of Austen's writing: "Mr. Bennet was so odd a mixture of quick *parts,* sarcastic *humour, reserve,* and *caprice,* that the experience of three and twenty years had been insufficient to make his wife understand his character. *Her* mind was less difficult to develope. She was a woman of mean *understanding,* little *information,* and uncertain *temper*" (italics, except "her," are mine). Seven large, conceptual nouns, with some accompanying adjectives, carry the content of this passage. And while this is perhaps a slightly exaggerated example, it is not too far from the norm for the narrative voice of *Pride and Prejudice.* Against this norm two deviations can be played. Characters who employ highly particularized language are usually betraying low intelligence, vulgarity, or both. On the other hand, Austen is aware of the potential dullness of an excessively abstract vocabulary and alert to the fact that, if one is going to rely heavily on conceptual terms, one had better be able to handle them with force and precision. (In the passage cited the needle-sharp precision of the vocabulary, combined with a crisp, balanced sentence structure to be discussed later, generates a sense of intellectual vitality and prevents ponderousness.) Thus, characters may betray undesirable habits of mind by overdoing the use of abstract terms, or using them improperly or unskillfully.

Austen prefers low-keyed to emphatic language. Understatement is more characteristic of her narrative voice than the reverse, and characters who employ hyperbolic language—who refer to "agonies" rather than "sorrows," who are in "raptures" rather than "happy," who become "furious" rather than "angry"—are suspect. She almost never employs metaphors, and thus when characters do so it becomes conspicuous—usually in a negative way, although the "blindness" metaphor mentioned in chapter 5 is a rare exception to this rule. (The distrust of metaphor is probably another inheritance from the neoclassical age, when Dryden, Pope, et al. reacted against what they considered the metaphoric excesses of Donne and others of the previous generation.) Her language tends to be rather formal. There are few colloquial words or expressions in the authorial voice, so that their appearance in the speech of a character often tells us something about him.

An important feature of Austen's sentence structure is a rather heavy reliance on passive, indirect, and/or impersonal constructions, as opposed to straightforward subject-active verb-object structures:

> It is a truth universally acknowledged [rather than "everyone believes"] that a single man in possession of a good fortune, must be in want of [rather than "needs"] a wife.
> *However little known the feelings* or views *of such a man may be* on his first entering a neighborhood, *this truth is so well fixed* in the minds of the surrounding families, *that he is considered as the rightful property* of some one or other of their daughters. (italics mine)

A character's use of a large number of more "active" constructions may be significant. On the other hand, Austen is alert to the weakening effect of excessive indirectness and passivity on style and she can exploit it to reveal traits of character.

Balanced phrasing is an extremely important element in Austen's style. It is her skill at handling balance, antithesis, and similar devices that gives her writing much of the incisiveness that is its hallmark. (Here, too, she harks back to her neoclassical heritage: the neatly balanced periods of Johnson or Gibbon; the heavy use of balance, antithesis, and chiasmus in the heroic couplets of Dryden and Pope.) She is fond of both two-part balanced or antithetical structures, and also of slightly longer series. The description of Mrs. Bennet quoted earlier, for example, finishes as follows: "She was a woman of *mean under-standing, little information,* and *uncertain temper.* When she was *discontented* she fancied herself *nervous.* The *business* of her life was to get her daughters married; its *solace* was visiting and news" (italics mine). Sentences 2 and 3 demonstrate two-part structures—an antithetical one in sentence 3. In the first sentence, we have a three-part series. These kinds of structures work beautifully in the narrative voice, and for a chosen few of her characters. Sometimes, however, characters who attempt to employ them will mismanage them, and the mishandlings can serve as characterizing devices.

SOME CHARACTERS' VERBAL STYLES AND WHAT THEY TELL US

One of the more obviously distinctive verbal styles in *Pride and Prejudice* is that of the bookish, cerebral Mary Bennet. Here is the speech that Mary makes to Elizabeth Bennet on the subject of their sister Lydia's running off, without benefit of matrimony, with Mr. Wickham:

> "This is a most unfortunate affair; and will probably be much talked of. But we must stem the tide of malice, and pour into the wounded bosoms of each other, the balm of sisterly consolation . . . Unhappy as the event must be for Lydia, we may draw from it this useful lesson; that loss of virtue in a female is irretrievable—that one false step involves her in endless ruin—that her reputation is no less brittle than it is beautiful—and that she cannot be too much guarded in her behavior towards the undeserving of the other sex. (289)

The coldly pompous moralizing of this speech is enhanced by several verbal devices. In the first place, there are no less than three metaphors—"stem the tide of malice," "pour into the wounded bosoms of each other, the balm of sisterly consolation," "no less brittle than it is beautiful"—in as many sentences. And these metaphors are of a flowery, "literary" quality entirely inappropriate to the situation at hand. (Just *how* "literary" they are will become apparent in the chapter on Austen's use of literary allusion that follows.) Second, there is the too-heavy reliance on balanced sentence structure: four exactly balanced clauses in a row in the last sentence, the balanced structure emphasized by the rhetorical repetition of the "that" (cf. "Mr. Bennet was so odd a mixture of quick parts, sarcastic humour, reserve, and caprice"). There is the indirectness created by the inverted structure of "pour into the wounded bosoms of each other, the balm of sisterly consolation." Finally there is the inaccurate use of highfalutin abstract terms in "endless ruin" (the term *ruin* is an absolute: what other kind of ruin could there be?). The speech sounds not like the spoken word but like (not very good) writing; and Mary's verbal style is the reflection of a mind that can see a sister's tragedy as if it were a moral exemplum from one of her "great books." Indeed, Austen describes Mary's remarks as "moral extractions" (like the "extracts" Mary makes from her books) "from the evil before them."

The speech on pride and vanity (20) quoted in a previous chapter reveals many of the same characteristics. In addition to the "literary" quality provided by Mary's borrowing from Adam Smith, one notes the overelaborately balanced structure of "that [pride] is very common indeed, that human nature is particularly prone to it, and that there are very few of us who do not cherish a feeling of self-complacency on the score of some quality or other." One also notes that all three of Mary's clauses *say* the same thing: she is unnecessarily multiplying words in order to create balance, and she achieves verbosity instead of vivacity. Another example of her excessive and often incorrect use of abstract terms is provided by her contribution to the family debate on Elizabeth's walking to Netherfield to see the ailing Jane Bennet, also quoted earlier (32). Mary prefaces her argument by saying, "I admire the activity of your benevolence" (rather than, say, "I appreciate your feeling for Jane"), and buries the emotional issue at stake under a mound of abstractions. Moreover, she cannot even choose her conceptual terms correctly: "benevolence" is hardly the appropriate term for what one feels for her favorite sister.

Verbal Styles

An overly abstract vocabulary, not well handled, verbosity, heavily rhetorical sentence structures, the excessively "literary" quality imparted by the frequent use of metaphor and literary "borrowings"— all of these cooperate to make up Mary's special voice. And the voice thus created is the perfect expression of Mary's role in the novel's thematic patterns. It is an important vehicle for establishing her, in her pedantic intellectualism and cold rationality, as one of the novel's representatives of an excess of "art" in the art–nature dialectic. Every time she opens her mouth Mary reinforces her thematic role by her verbal style. Not only what she says, but the way she expresses it, defines her symbolic function in the novel.

With Mary's voice echoing in our minds' ears, it is interesting to turn to her opposite, Lydia Bennet. When Lydia has been finally married off to Wickham and visits her family at Longbourn, she favors Elizabeth, over Elizabeth's protests, with an account of the morning of her wedding day:

> "La! You are so strange! But I must tell you how it went off. We were married, you know, at St. Clement's because Wickham's lodgings were in that parish. And it was settled that we should all be there by eleven o'clock. My uncle and aunt and I were to go together; and the others were to meet us at the church. Well, Monday morning came, and I was in such a fuss! I was so afraid you know that something would happen to put it off, and then I should have gone quite distracted . . . Well, and so we breakfasted at ten as usual. I thought it would never be over; for, by the bye, you are to understand, that my uncle and aunt were horrid unpleasant all the time I was with them. If you'll believe me, I did not once put my foot out of doors, though I was there a fortnight . . . Well, and so just as the carriage came to the door, my uncle was called away upon business to that horrid man Mr. Stone. And then, you know, when once they get together, there is no end of it . . . But, luckily, he came back again in ten minutes' time." (319)

Lydia's vocabulary abounds in colloquialisms: "La!," "in such a fuss," "put it off," "get together," "no end of it." Her language is highly emphatic; we note "I should have gone quite distracted," and her all-purpose term of disapprobation, "horrid," as well as the large number of exclamations. She favors rather particularized language ("I did not once put my foot out of doors" rather than "I never went out"). Sentence structure is very simple and direct. It is also very ungrammatical. Sentence fragments and run-on sentences dominate the passage. There are no principles of subordination, grammatical or logical, in the speech. Thoughts tumble out as they occur to Lydia and are strung together, equally weighted, with "ands." The only real punctuation in the speech occurs when Lydia must pause for breath and fetches up with a "well" or "however."

Similar traits can be observed in Lydia's speech elsewhere. The vulgar exclamation, "Lord!" punctuates her speeches regularly. The particularized "You will laugh" or "I was ready to die of laughter" (note also the hyperbolic quality of the latter) are preferred to "You will be amused" or "I was amused." Indeed, in Lydia's case, emphasis and particularity of expression extend to "body language": she "yawns," "gapes," and "stretches" with frequency, for instance. Her monologue in the coach when she and Kitty have met Jane and Elizabeth on the latter's return from London (221) displays the same structural nonpatterns seen in the speech about her wedding day. While Mary Bennet's voice displayed a series of characteristics designed to reinforce her position as a representative of "art," Lydia's exclamations, overemphasis, particularity, colloquialism, and loose structures become the signs of her excesses in the direction of "nature." The disorganized emotionalism of her mind is mirrored in the verbal turmoil of her speech.

Mr. Collins's verbal style is in some ways like that of Mary Bennet. As we have seen earlier, he is guilty of metaphor. He urges Mr. Bennet to leave Lydia to "reap the fruit of her . . . heinous offence" (297) after her elopement with Wickham, and we recall the resounding cliché of the "olive branch" in his first letter. Mr. Collins also revels in the cliché per se, metaphorical or otherwise. His house is never his house but his "humble parsonage" or "humble abode"—three times in the course of one dialogue (66–67). He is also verbose: in the same conversation Lady Catherine does not "approve" of his sermons but is "graciously pleased to approve" of them. She "has condescended to advise" him and "vouchsafed to suggest" improvements in his house. Miss De Bourgh even "condescends to drive by [his] humble abode." He favors lengthy, balanced sentence structures. In proposing to Elizabeth he declares that "It does not appear to me that my hand is unworthy your acceptance, or that the establishment I can offer would be any other than highly desirable. My situation in life, my connections with the family of De Bourgh, and my relationship with your own, are circumstances highly in my favour" (108). His sentence structure is also frequently indirect to the point of absurdity: "The garden in which stands [his] humble abode is separated only by a lane from Rosings Park" (66). "Twice has [Lady Catherine] condescended to give [him] her opinion" on matrimony (105). And he has his own particular device for creating indirection: the double negative construction. The rector of a parish "must make such an agreement for tythes as may be beneficial to himself and not offensive to his patron. He must write his own sermons; and the time that remains will not be too much for his parish duties, and the care and improvement of his dwelling, which he cannot be excused from making as comfortable as possible" (101).

We observe also that the double negatives of the "proposal" passage quoted above help to undermine any "punch" that the balanced phrasing might have given. The passage on the duties of the rector above reveals another special Collins-ism: his tendency to organize his speeches under numerical headings, as he must do in his sermons. Similarly, his proposal to Elizabeth begins, "My reasons for marrying are, first, that I think it a right thing for every clergyman . . . to set the example of matrimony in his parish. Secondly, that I am convinced it will add very greatly to my happiness; and thirdly . . . that it is the particular advice and recommendation of the very noble lady whom I have the honour of calling patroness" (105). As is the case with Mary's verbal style, Collins's tricks of speech are all of the sort that render him stiff, stilted, and stultifying; and they thus complement his role as one of the novel's representatives of an excess of "art."

As a final example from among the subordinate characters in the novel, Mrs. Bennet is not to be resisted. One of her most typical speeches is her account to Mr. Bennet of the first Meryton assembly:

> "Oh! my dear Mr. Bennet . . . we have had a most delightful evening, a most excellent ball. I wish you had been there. Jane was so admired, nothing could be like it. Every body said how well she looked; and Mr. Bingley thought her quite beautiful, and danced with her twice. Only think of *that*, my dear; he actually danced with her twice; and she was the only creature in the room that he asked a second time . . . he seemed quite struck with Jane as she was going down the dance. So, he enquired who she was, and got introduced, and asked her for the two next . . . I am quite delighted with him. He is so excessively handsome! and his sisters are charming women. I never in my life saw any thing more elegant than their dresses . . . But I can assure you . . . that Lizzy does not lose much by not suiting *his* [Darcy's] fancy; for he is a most disagreeable, horrid man, not at all worth pleasing. So high and so conceited that there was no enduring him! He walked here, and he walked there, fancying himself so very great . . . I quite detest the man." (12–13)

The abrupt, staccato rhythms of the speech are among its most conspicuous features. Mrs. Bennet habitually speaks in short sentences, usually with a subject-verb-object structure, or in compound sentences with clauses of an equally direct construction that have the same effect. Her language is consistently hyperbolic. Jane is so admired that "nothing could be like it." Bingley is "excessively handsome," and she never in her life saw "any thing more elegant" than his sisters' dresses. Darcy, on the other hand, is "horrid" (we see where Lydia derived her fondness for the term). She "quite detests" him. Exclamations abound. The vocabulary is often colloquial. Bingley is "quite struck" with Jane, but Elizabeth does not "lose much by not suiting [Darcy's] fancy." One notes also the tendency toward particularity in speech. Mr. Darcy "walked here and he walked there." I, at least, envision Mrs. Bennet acting out Darcy's haughtiness with "body language" here, striding back and forth, hands behind her back perhaps, and head erected, in imitation. One imagines "body language" to be characteristic of Mrs.

Verbal Styles

Bennet in a high degree. Her last speech (378), upon her flabbergasted receipt of the news of Elizabeth's engagement to Darcy, is actually introduced by stage directions telling us that she "fidgets about in her chair," "gets up," and "sits down again." It also contains nineteen exclamations, and the average sentence length is about six words. Elsewhere, Mrs. Bennet shows a fondness for metaphor. Her metaphors, however, have the reverse effect from those of her daughter Mary. Where Mary's are flowery and "literary" sounding, Mrs. Bennet's are homely and often rather vulgar. She does not get a "wink of sleep" when she is emotionally overcharged (306). She has "liked a red coat very well" in her youth (29). She fears the Collinses will turn her out of Longbourn before Mr. Bennet is "cold in his grave" (287). What we are getting in Mrs. Bennet, of course, is an older and shriller version of her daughter Lydia; the same mindless emotionalism tinctured with the sharpness of socioeconomic anxiety. An excess of "nature," once again, is embodied in an excessively "natural" verbal style.

When we come to the two major characters, Elizabeth and Darcy, who are closer to the novel's moral and social norms, we find verbal styles that more nearly approximate that of the narrative voice. Both Elizabeth and Darcy employ conceptual terms with frequency, and both do it well. Indeed, the verbal fluency and precision of their speech is one of the great delights of the novel. Elizabeth can impale a character with the same sort of verbal incisiveness that her author delights in. Mr. Collins, she says to Jane à propos of his engagement to Charlotte Lucas, is "a conceited, pompous, narrow-minded, silly man; you know he is, as well as I do; and you must feel, as I do, that the woman who marries him, cannot have a proper way of thinking" (135). Darcy, in the conversation on Bingley's "precipitance," can enjoy playing upon the distinction between persuasion and conviction:

[Elizabeth:] "To yield readily—easily—to the *persuasion* of a friend is no merit with you."
[Darcy:] "To yield without conviction is no compliment to the understanding of either." (50)

Both Elizabeth and Darcy can employ balanced and antithetical sentence structures effectively. In her argument with Jane over Charlotte Lucas's engagement Elizabeth goes on to say that Jane must not "endeavour to persuade yourself or me, that selfishness is prudence, and insensibility of danger, security for happiness." In the conversation on precipitance she asks Bingley, "Would Mr. Darcy then consider the rashness of your original intention as atoned for by your obstinacy in adhering to it?" Continuing the same debate, Darcy dryly asks, "Will it not be advisable, before we proceed on this subject, to arrange with rather more precision the degree of importance which is to appertain to this request, as well as the degree of intimacy subsisting between the parties?"

There are some interesting differences between Elizabeth's and Darcy's verbal styles, however. While Darcy is not verbose or excessively indirect, he tends to speak at somewhat greater length and to employ somewhat longer and less direct constructions than Elizabeth does. Elizabeth, while she frequently constructs quite sophisticated sentences and is far from Mrs. Bennet's excessive brevity and simplicity in structure, does employ short, direct constructions at times. The differences between Elizabeth's and Darcy's styles emerge most clearly, of course, in their conversations with one another. A typical exchange will often consist of two or three rather lengthy and complex sentences from Darcy, followed by a brisk, direct one- or two-liner from Elizabeth. We have touched in another chapter on the conversation at Netherfield on feminine "accomplishments" (39–40). Here Darcy claims that he knows no more than half a dozen "really accomplished" women, and Miss Bingley seconds him with her list of the requisites for the truly accomplished lady. Darcy then takes over the conversation, saying

"All this she must possess . . . and to all this she must add something more substantial, in the improvement of her mind by extensive reading."
[Elizabeth:] "I am no longer surprised by your knowing *only* six accomplished women. I rather wonder now at your knowing *any*."
"Are you so severe upon your own sex, as to doubt the possibility of all this?"

Verbal Styles

"*I* never saw such a woman. *I* never saw such capacity, and taste, and application, and elegance, as you describe, united."

Darcy's long, inverted, rather passive sentences are neatly contrasted with Elizabeth's directness and vigor. Similarly, in another of their verbal battles (57–58) Elizabeth says to Darcy

"I hope I never ridicule what is wise or good. Follies and nonsense, whims and inconsistencies *do* divert me, I own, and I laugh at them whenever I can.—But these, I suppose, are precisely what you are without."

"Perhaps that is not possible for any one. But it has been the study of my life to avoid those weaknesses which often expose a strong understanding to ridicule."

"Such as vanity and pride."

"Yes, vanity is a weakness indeed. But pride—where there is a real superiority of mind, pride will be always under good regulation."

As the conversation draws to a close Darcy admits that his "temper would perhaps be called resentful"; his "good opinion, once lost is lost forever":

"*That* is a failing indeed!"—cried Elizabeth. "Implacable resentment *is* a shade in a character. But you have chosen your fault well.—I really cannot *laugh* at it. You are safe with me."

"There is, I believe, in every disposition a tendency to some particular evil, a natural defect, which not even the best education can overcome."

"And *your* defect is a propensity to hate every body."

"And yours," he replied with a smile, "is wilfully to misunderstand them."

We should observe here that, while the two verbal styles are distinctive, neither character is *confined* to his particular one. Elizabeth can produce her sentence on "follies and nonsense," and Darcy can cap Elizabeth's one-liner with one of his own at the end of their exchange.

Although she does not overdo it, Elizabeth tends to speak somewhat more emphatically than Darcy does. We note the exclamations and the fairly large number of italicized words in the speeches of hers that have been quoted above, for example. Finally, Elizabeth will occasionally employ a colloquial phrase in her conversation. Interestingly, when she does so, it often seems to be directed at Darcy, as a sort of challenge. Thus, when forced by Charlotte Lucas to perform at the pianoforte, she remarks, "gravely glancing at Mr. Darcy," "there is a fine old saying, which every body here is of course familiar with— 'Keep your breath to cool your porridge,'—and I shall keep mine to swell my song" (24). And in conversation with Darcy and Colonel Fitzwilliam at Rosings, she says, to the latter and at the former: "Your cousin will give you a very pretty notion of me, and teach you not to believe a word I say" (174).

As I have remarked above, the speeches of Elizabeth and Darcy, especially their verbal battles, are some of the best things in the novel. The elegant precision of language, the pleasing "sound" of well-constructed sentences, and the contrast between different speech patterns produce the sort of witty vitality that one finds in the couplets of Pope and in the best scenes of Congreve or Sheridan. In addition to being delightful in themselves, moreover, the speeches of Elizabeth and Darcy "work" thematically. Elizabeth's brisk and vivid voice, with its slight touches of colloquialism, is the verbal manifestation of the natural "ease and liveliness" of her character. Darcy's slower moving, more formal style reflects the "judgement, information and knowledge of the world," the higher degree of "art" that he represents.[11]

Our enjoyment of the verbal eccentricities of a Mr. Collins or a Mrs. Bennet, or of the verbal brilliance of an argument between Elizabeth and Darcy, then, is always something more than an end in itself. To an extraordinary degree, Austen makes verbal style thematically functional. Perhaps of no other artist could it be said any *more* truly that, as far as the handling of language is concerned, the medium literally is the message. Considering the use of verbal style in *Pride and Prejudice* we are brought to consider yet another manifestation of the beautiful economy of Austen's art.

9

—————— LITERARY ALLUSION
Some Backgrounds

The Austen family circle, as I have remarked earlier, was an extremely bookish group of folk. Austen's existing letters to family and friends are filled with references to literature ranging from Hannah More's *Practical Piety* to Byron's *The Corsair;* from Fielding's *Tom Jones* to Lord Macartney's *Journal of the Embassy to China.* Reading, and talk of what they read, was clearly an integral part of the Austen way of life; and, as we noted in the previous chapter, various members of the family in addition to Jane enjoyed trying their hands at writing as well. The Austen group would appear to have been an intelligent, lively, and critical lot, and they greatly enjoyed a laugh at bad writing, or lapses or idiosyncracies on the parts of favorite authors, as well as appreciating good stuff. This led, as one might imagine, to the production of tongue-in-cheek imitations—some of which Austen's brothers James and Henry shared with a wider audience when they brought out a literary periodical at Oxford in 1789–90.

Austen's own literary career begins with imitations and burlesques designed to entertain the family circle. There is, among other juvenilia, a takeoff on Oliver Goldsmith's *History of England,* in which a "partial, prejudiced and ignorant historian" exculpates the notorious Richard III with relentless illogic:

The character of this prince has been very severely treated by historians, but as he was a *York*, I am rather inclined to suppose him a respectable man. It has indeed been confidently asserted that he killed his two nephews and his wife; but it has also been declared that he did *not* kill his two nephews, which I am inclined to believe true; and if this is the case, it may also be affirmed that he did not kill his wife. (*Minor Works*, 141)

There is *Love and Freindship*, an hilarious burlesque of the excesses of contemporary sentimental and Gothic fiction, in which one of the heroines expires after having fainted fifteen times in succession during a particularly harrowing emotional crisis, leaving her confidante with the following moral admonition:

> Beware of fainting fits . . . Though at the time they may be refreshing and agreeable, yet believe me they will in the end, if too often repeated and at improper seasons, prove destructive to your constitution . . . Beware of swoons, dear Laura . . . A frenzy fit is not one quarter so pernicious; it is an exercise to the body, and, if not too violent, is, I dare say, conducive to health in its consequences—run mad as often as you choose—but do not faint. (*Minor Works*, 102)

The recently discovered *Sir Charles Grandison: Or The Happy Man* is a largely comic dramatic version of Samuel Richardson's *Sir Charles Grandison*—a novel about which much is to be said in its connection with *Pride and Prejudice* later in this chapter.

The fact that Austen begins her writing life as a satirist–imitator is of very great importance indeed. For one thing, it is almost certain that her first three novels—*Northanger Abbey, Sense and Sensibility,* and *Pride and Prejudice*—go back to prototypes close in time and manner to the juvenilia and that they arrived at the states in which we know them as the results of processes of extensive and probably repeated revision. Certain features of the novels as we have them are often alleged by critics to be traces of these prototypes. And many critics, myself among them, believe that there is a hard core of satire or corrective imitation of some sort of literature at the center of every one of the novels. (Even in the unfinished *Sanditon*, Austen's last novel, at least two major characters are clearly meant to be recognized as types based on the fiction of the day, and one of them—Sir Edward Denham—is treated with surprisingly broad satiric touches.) More important, all of the novels, while they are not (except for parts of *Northanger Abbey*) directed *at* literature in the manner of most of the juvenilia, nevertheless display the practice, analogous to that of the parodist, of exploiting an audience's knowledge of popular works. Austen's is a highly allusive art. She uses verbal echoes, character types, themes, and situations that she can, and does, expect her early nineteenth-century audience to recognize, constantly. And literary allusions become, in a very real sense, part of the "meaning" of her works. Her contemporaries' sense of what her novels "said" would have come in part from referring them, as their allusive nature encourages, back to their analogues in the literary milieu of the eighteenth and early nineteenth centuries. We as twentieth-century readers may miss a whole dimension of her writing unless we attempt to read her novels in relation to this milieu. Not to do so is rather like trying to appreciate Pope's *The Rape of the Lock* or Joyce's *Ulysses* without any knowledge of classical epics, or Dryden's *Absalom and Achitophel* or Faulkner's *Absalom, Absalom!* without knowledge of the biblical story to which they allude.

In *Pride and Prejudice* allusion is of at least two sorts. On one level, there are numerous "local" allusions—usually verbal echoes—that perform several different kinds of functions for the alert reader. On another, and more important, plane *Pride and Prejudice* as a whole is patterned in a very special way upon stories employing a popular character type and situation—what I have called the "patrician hero" motif—from eighteenth- and early nineteenth-century fiction. And Austen's handling of this motif bears an important relation to her ethical and social themes.

A FEW LOCAL ALLUSIONS

To begin at the beginning, the novel's title is itself a form of allusion. The phrase "pride and prejudice" crops up with very great frequency in various types of eighteenth- and nineteenth-century literature. Perhaps the most dramatic occurrence of the expression comes in the concluding chapter of Fanny Burney's *Cecilia* (1782) where the manifold sufferings of the hero and heroine are said by one of the characters to have been "the result of PRIDE and PREJUDICE . . . Yet . . . if to PRIDE and PREJUDICE you owe your miseries, so wonderfully is good and evil balanced, that to PRIDE and PREJUDICE you will also owe their termination." As R. W. Chapman's notes to the Oxford edition of *Pride and Prejudice* and countless contributions to *Notes and Queries* and the *London Times Literary Supplement* testify, however, the phrase and variants of it appear in a variety of other works, including Richardson's *Sir Charles Grandison* and the *Sermons, Chiefly Designed to Elucidate Some of the Leading Doctrines of the Gospel* (1804) of Austen's cousin Edward Cooper (who recommends "an humble and a teachable mind, divested of prejudice and pride"). In the passage from John Mason's *Self-Knowledge* quoted earlier in this study there is, we recall, another variant. The early nineteenth-century reader could not help hearing mental echoes in simply looking at the title of *Pride and Prejudice.*

Austen frequently chooses phrases or terms that are commonplaces in the literature of her period for the titles of her works. The early *Love and Friendship, Sense and Sensibility,* and *Persuasion* all have titles of this sort—as did *First Impressions,* the earlier work that was the prototype for *Pride and Prejudice,* according to family tradition. The effect of employing such titles is to highlight the allusive nature of Austen's writing. When one picks up a book entitled "*Pride and Prejudice,*" and recognizes a phrase borrowed from the stock properties of the literature of the day, one is being conditioned, in a subtle way, with regard to the contents to follow. This book, such a title implies, exists within a certain literary context. It has relations, which may prove worth pondering upon, to the world of literature as well as to the world of life outside. The choice of the title of *Pride and Prejudice,* then, is an artistic strategy (just how consciously arrived at is a question incapable of settlement) that prepares the reader for a literature-oriented book—an intimation that is amply fulfilled as he reads on.

Literary Allusion

The famous opening sentence of *Pride and Prejudice* also contains a literary allusion of sorts. The narrator's phrase, "it is a truth universally acknowledged," is meant to recall the language of philosophical discourse to Austen's audience. Similar references to the *consensus gentium,* in very similar language, are common in philosophical works known to Austen and her contemporaries. "It is a received opinion that language has no other end but the communicating ideas," says Bishop Berkeley in his *Principles of Human Knowledge* (1710). " 'Tis universally allowed, that the capacity of the mind is limited," writes David Hume in his *Treatise of Human Nature* (1739). And Adam Smith, in the *Theory of Moral Sentiments* (1759), which Elizabeth and Mary Bennet have both read, remarks that when "general rules . . . are universally acknowledged and established, . . . we frequently appeal to them as to the standards of judgement." By actually echoing the language associated with Hume, Smith, and other prestigious philosophers of the day, Austen enhances the ironic contrast between the beginning and the end of her opening sentence. Her wit, delightful as it is to the twentieth-century reader, would be even sharper to an audience nurtured on the works of Smith and Hume, as they watched what appeared to be the beginning of a philosophical proposition turn into burlesque. "It is a truth universally acknowledged [how impressive] that a single man in possession of a good fortune [well . . .] must be in want of [yes?]—a wife [?!]."

In addition to sharpening the wit of the narrative voice, local allusion is also employed as a characterizing device by Austen. Characters whom she respects may echo sources known to her audience in interesting and appropriate ways, as signs that they are intelligent and well-read. Thus, we have seen in a previous chapter that Elizabeth Bennet can make an apposite and witty reference to Adam Smith's *Theory of Moral Sentiments,* when she says of Darcy's behavior, "I could easily forgive *his* pride, if he had not mortified *mine."* Darcy, too, can echo well-known works appropriately. In the conversation on precipitancy (47–49) Mr. Bingley remarks amiably of his writing that "my ideas flow so rapidly that I have not time to express them—by which means my letters sometimes convey no ideas at all to my correspondents." Elizabeth praises Bingley's modesty: "your humility, Mr. Bingley . . . must disarm reproof." Darcy replies that "nothing is more deceitful than the appearance of humility" and adds that it is, in Bingley's case, a form of "indirect boast," Bingley being in fact rather proud of his "rapidity of thought and carelessness of execution" in epistolary and other matters. As R. W. Chapman has pointed out in the notes to the Oxford *Pride and Prejudice,* Darcy's shrewd psychological assessment here recalls a passage from Austen's favorite, Samuel Johnson, who is quoted by Boswell in the *Life of Johnson* as making a similar observation on human nature: "All censure of a man's self is oblique praise."

On the other hand, characters of whom Austen disapproves may be made to betray pretentiousness or dullness of mind or both by excessive and/or inept borrowing. Mary Bennet is the novel's undisputed champion in this respect, as might be expected. We have seen earlier that Elizabeth's appropriation from Adam Smith in the conversation on Darcy's pride triggers a lengthy, uncalled-for, and ponderously worded dissertation on the distinction between vanity and pride in which Mary's remarks sound suspiciously like "extracts" from Smith. Mary outdoes herself in the speech, quoted in the previous chapter, on Lydia's elopement with Wickham (289). Early in the speech she introduces the metaphor "we must pour into the wounded bosoms of each other, the balm of sisterly consolation." Her language here is not only impossibly inflated in itself; it is also borrowed from Richardson's *Sir Charles Grandison,* where the heroine says to a young friend in an emotional crisis, "now, my dear, I conjure you, by the friendship that is between us, the *more* than sisterly friendship, open your whole heart to me; and renounce me, if it be in my power to heal the wounds of your mind, and I do not pour into them the balm of friendly love."[12] Later in the same speech Mary's remark that a woman's "reputation is no less brittle than it is beautiful" is taken from Fanny Burney's *Evelina,* where it is said that "nothing is so delicate as the reputation of a woman: it is at once the most brittle and most beautiful of all human things."[13] Thus we have recognizable "extracts" in two sentences.

Austen also uses the "echo" technique to reinforce our impressions of Mr. Collins's character. His hope that Mr. Bennet will not "reject the proffered olive branch" of his letter is clichéd enough even to the twentieth-century reader. To a reader brought up on the novels of Samuel Richardson the cliché effect would be even more powerful. The term "olive branch" is a favorite with a clergyman, the Reverend Elias Brand, in Richardson's *Clarissa*. And in *Sir Charles Grandison* the heroine urges the estranged Lady Clementina della Poretta to be reconciled to her family by saying, "let your sister Harriet prevail upon you not to reject the offered olive branch."[14]

This is but a sampling of the "local" allusions and their functions in *Pride and Prejudice*. There are many others that cannot be included here, and the interested reader is referred to the bibliography on literary allusion given elsewhere in this study. It is, I hope, evident that the more one knows about its literary milieu, the more fun—and the more meaningful—*Pride and Prejudice* is for him. It is now time to turn to the larger allusive pattern upon which *Pride and Prejudice* as a whole is based.

PUTTING DOWN THE PATRICIAN HERO

For our purposes it is the novels of Samuel Richardson and Fanny Burney that give definitive formulation to the character type I have referred to as the "patrician hero." Richardson's work was, as must be obvious to the reader by now, extremely well known to Austen. The presence of numerous allusions throughout her fiction, the burlesque *Sir Charles Grandison: Or, The Happy Man*, references in her letters, and biographical data testify to her thorough familiarity with his productions. His *Sir Charles Grandison* was the favorite novel of her mother. All three of Richardson's novels—*Pamela*, *Clarissa*, and *Sir Charles Grandison*—revolve around the relationships between men who are wealthy and highly born society figures and young women who are their social inferiors in varying degrees. The heroes of the first two novels, while glamorous and impressive figures, are both flawed. The rakish Mr. B—— of *Pamela* must be reformed by the virtuous Pamela's resolute defense of her virginity. In *Clarissa* the talented and charming Lovelace is a compulsive seducer who is beyond redemption and who ultimately destroys both Clarissa and himself. In *Sir Charles Grandison*, however, Richardson set himself the task of depicting a role model for the English Christian gentleman—"a man of religion and virtue; of liveliness and spirit; accomplished and agreeable; happy in himself, and a blessing to others."[15] *Sir Charles Grandison* is the story of the love affair between Sir Charles and Miss Harriet Byron. Harriet is a pretty and virtuous young woman of modest but respectable rank and fortune. On a visit to London she is abducted by the villainous Sir Hargrave Pollexfen and carried off to be threatened with a clandestine marriage or a Fate Worse Than Death. She is rescued from his clutches by Sir Charles, who comes riding up out of nowhere on a white horse and carries her off to safety. She remains at his house, at his sister's invitation, for an extended visit and is soon deeply in love with him. After seven volumes of heart burning and anxiety on her part they are at last married.

Sir Charles is as handsome as a matinée idol and possessed of an "address" that is irresistible to women. At least five are in love with him in the course of the story, and one —the tempestuous Italian, Lady Clementina della Poretta—literally goes mad with frustrated passion. He is a man of great wealth, splendid houses, large holdings of land. Possessed of a strong sense of noblesse oblige, however, he regards his fortune and position in life as Christian trusts. He is active and remarkably competent in the management of his estates, all of which he personally supervises. And as a landlord and employer he is notable for his justice, benevolence, and concern for those under his stewardship. Morally, he is a shining example to mankind. (Richardson even averred to acquaintances that Sir Charles was a virgin when he married.) His manners, to both his equals and his inferiors, are perfection.

If all of this were not enough to make the reader feel a little bit "sick and wicked"—to borrow Austen's own phrase regarding the effect of too-perfect characters upon herself—Sir Charles is surrounded by a little court of aficionados, male and female, who constantly call attention to his excellence. Their incessant praise, their attempts at emulation, their deference to his opinions and advice create an atmosphere unintentionally suggestive almost of sycophancy that is likely to become trying for most readers. One of the most frequent manifestations of this admiration is a tendency on the part of his family, friends, and acquaintances to put the management of their affairs into his hands while they are living and to make him executor of their estates when they die. He extricates a sister and an uncle from improper romantic entanglements and provides both with suitable mates. He reconciles quarrelling relatives, administers trusts, and acts as guardian to orphans. At a high point in his career Harriet Byron lists some seven persons or families whose affairs of various sorts Sir Charles is happily rearranging.

Of all Sir Charles's worshipers Harriet is (with the possible exception of the love-maddened Lady Clementina) the most devoted. She refers to him as her "monitor," and indeed their relationship resembles that of an adoring pupil to an idolized teacher rather more than that of lover to lover. She is in love with him long before she knows that she has any hope of a return, and much of the novel revolves around her doubts regarding his feelings and hesitations regarding her own worth. When at (very great) length she has proved herself worthy of him and Sir Charles marries her, she is nearly overcome with gratitude. She prays God to make her properly "thankful for such a friend, protector, director, husband! Increase with my gratitude to THEE, my merits to him" (vol. 7, letter 60, 316). And in her last letter to her grandmother she writes

> My single heart, methinks, is not big enough to contain the gratitude which such a lot demands. Let the over-flowings of your pious joy, my dearest grandmamma, join with my thankfulness, in paying part of the immense debt for
> > Your undeservedly happy
> > Harriet Grandison (vol. 8, letter 62, 325)

Evidence from the letters, novels, juvenilia, and biography shows that Austen was as familiar with the work of Fanny Burney as she was with that of Richardson. The three novels that Fanny Burney published before 1813—*Evelina, Cecilia,* and *Camilla*—all deal with involvements between Grandisonian society figures and heroines who are more or less on probation until the ends of their stories. *Cecilia* is often cited as a source for certain features of *Pride and Prejudice.* The most important Burneyan manifestation of the patrician hero for our purposes, however, is Lord Orville, the hero of *Evelina.* In this novel Evelina Anvile, the heroine, is actually the daughter and legitimate heiress of the wealthy Sir John Belmont, but her birth is not acknowledged until the conclusion of the story, and she has been brought up in a modest country rectory in the guardianship of the Reverend Mr. Villars, a wise and kindly clergyman. At the beginning of the novel she makes a trip to London, where she meets the handsome and wealthy Orville, with whom she promptly falls in love. Evelina is continually being embarrassed by the social errors to which her lack of knowledge of the world lead her, as well as by the vulgarity of a group of relatives with whom she is forced to associate; it seems impossible to her that she could ever win Lord Orville's love. Ultimately, however, she is found worthy of this paragon.

Lord Orville is clearly a literary descendant of Sir Charles Grandison. He seems, to Evelina and Fanny Burney, "formed as a pattern for his fellow creatures, as a model of perfection."[16] Evelina reports after their first encounter that "His conversation was sensible and spirited; his air, and address were open and noble; his manners gentle, attentive and infinitely engaging; his person is all elegance, and his countenance, the most animated and expressive I have ever seen" (33). He is, moreover, a model of social and moral rectitude, and he becomes a mentor to his heroine in the manner of Sir Charles Grandison. Evelina seeks his advice in delicate and difficult matters, and she receives it with gushing gratitude. Orville also shows a touch of the Grandisonian managerial talents. It is he who brings about the *eclairissement* with Sir John Belmont that establishes Evelina's paternity— and it is he who generously arranges for the settlement of half of her newly acquired fortune upon her illegitimate half-brother.

Evelina, like Harriet Byron, is embarrassingly aware of her good fortune in securing her patrician hero. When she learns that she is "the honoured choice of his noble heart," she writes, "my happiness seemed too infinite to be borne, and I wept, even bitterly I wept, from the excess of joy which overpowered me" (383). On the eve of her marriage she writes to Mr. Villars: "the thankfulness of my heart I must pour forth at our meeting . . . when my noble-minded, my beloved Lord Orville, presents to you the highly-honoured and thrice-happy Evelina" (438).

In the cases of both Orville and Sir Charles Grandison, over-emphasis on the heroes' perfection and excessive deference on the part of characters and authors alike tend to be counterproductive. The reader often inclines to respond to Fanny Burney's and Richardson's heroes as rather stuffy, even supercilious characters, rather than the engaging gentlemen their authors had in mind. Such feelings were not shared by a number of minor novelists of the period, however, for patrician heroes on the Burney–Richardson model are very popular in the lesser fiction of the eighteenth and nineteenth centuries. One finds in Thomas Hull's *The History of Sir William Harrington* (1771), for example, a hero clearly based on Sir Charles Grandison. And Anna Maria Porter's *The Lake of Killarney* (1804) contains a Mr. Charlemont who might have walked out of the pages of a Burneyan novel (and a scene that looks as if it were lifted from Burney's *Cecilia)*. The patrician hero, then, was a character type that the early nineteenth-century audience knew well. (Thackeray, at the middle of the nineteenth century, was relying on an audience's familiarity with the type in both his early sketch, "Catherine: A Story," and in his masterpiece, *Vanity Fair,* subtitled "A Novel without A Hero.")[17]

There is evidence in Austen's juvenilia that she herself was aware of the patrician hero as a fixture in the novels of the day and was amused by the excessive glamour and goodness characteristic of the type. In a sketch entitled "Jack and Alice," she produces Charles Adams, a young man "of so dazzling a Beauty that none but Eagles could look him in the face" (*Minor Works*, 13). When Charles attends a masquerade disguised, appropriately, as the sun, the beams that dart from his eyes are "so strong . . . that no one dared venture within half a mile of them" (13). (The references to Charles in terms of brilliance and radiance are probably designed specifically to recall *Sir Charles Grandison*: Richardson frequently uses the same sort of imagery in connection with his hero.)[18] Physical beauty, however, is the least of Charles's perfections. To quote his own words,

> "I imagine my Manners & Address to be of the most polished kind; there is a certain elegance, a peculiar sweetness in them that I never saw equalled, & cannot describe—Partiality aside, I am certainly more accomplished in every Language, every Science, every Art and every thing than any other person in Europe. My temper is even, my virtues innumerable, my self unparalleled." (25)

Thus Austen mocks the too-perfect hero not only by exaggeration but by having him do his own praise singing. The aura of superciliousness and conceit that surrounds a Sir Charles Grandison or Lord Orville in spite of their authors' intentions surfaces in the burlesque of "Jack and Alice." Not that Charles really needs to praise himself, however. The burlesque is continued by giving him not one but two heroines who grotesquely exaggerate both the inferiority and the devotion of Harriet and Evelina to their heroes. Lucy—daughter of a tailor and niece of an alehouse keeper—in the throes of her passion writes "a very kind letter" to Charles, "offering him with great tenderness my hand and heart"; but, alas, she receives "an angry and peremptory refusal" (21). Alice, the titular heroine of the piece, comes from a family of dipsomaniac gamblers whose propensities she shares. When she inherits an estate, her father proposes marriage with her to Charles. Charles replies: "What do you mean by wishing me to marry your daughter? Your Daughter Sir, is neither sufficiently beautifull, sufficiently amiable, sufficiently witty, nor sufficiently rich for me—. I expect nothing more in my wife than my wife will find in me—Perfection" (25–26).

We have seen, then, that the Burney–Richardson patrician hero was a character type well known to Austen's audience and recognized and satirically attacked by herself in at least one literary performance. Bearing these facts in mind, let us now turn to *Pride and Prejudice*—and to Fitzwilliam Darcy.

In his external circumstances and qualities Darcy is a "straight"—indeed a somewhat toned-down and more realistic version—of Sir Charles Grandison or Lord Orville, rather than a burlesque exaggeration such as Charles Adams. He is not a matinée idol, but he does possess a "fine tall person" and "handsome features" (10). His mental abilities are impressive. "Bingley was by no means deficient (in understanding)," we are told, but "Darcy was clever" (16). And Elizabeth, we remember, respects his "judgement, information and knowledge of the world" (312). Darcy's wealth and power do not reach such awesome proportions as those of Sir Charles Grandison, but he is a very wealthy man. (Ten thousand pounds clear *income*, from mostly landed property, implies an impressive amount of property.) He has clerical livings at his disposal, and he can buy Wickham out of debt and into a regiment. He marries a woman who is his social inferior, and who, like Fanny Burney's Evelina, has reason to be embarrassed by the vulgarity of some of her nearest relations.

In personality and behavior, however, Darcy is something else. In the depiction of his snobbery, his exaggerated ideas of the importance of his social advantages, his conceited determination to think well of himself and meanly of others, Austen is mounting an attack on the patrician hero. The scene, already discussed, where he hides behind his book in Elizabeth's presence in order not to risk "elevating" her with hopes of his hand makes Darcy seem a caricature of the (to their authors) modest Grandison and Orville. And the language of the first proposal scene sounds as if it might have come from a Charles Adams rather than from a Sir Charles Grandison, or a Lord Orville.

On two occasions, indeed, Darcy is quite specifically a caricature of Fanny Burney's Lord Orville. As Q. D. Leavis points out, the famous scene at the beginning of *Pride and Prejudice* where Darcy refuses Bingley's proposal of an introduction to Elizabeth Bennet parodies a similar one in *Evelina*.[19] When Orville and Evelina have just met, a friend of Evelina's overhears Orville discussing her in a manner that is not very flattering. She repeats the conversation to a heartsick Evelina, who records it in a letter to her guardian:

> A very gay looking young man stepping hastily up to (Orville), cried,
> "Why, my Lord, what have you done with your lovely partner?"
> "Nothing!" answered Lord Orville, with a smile and a shrug.
> "By Jove," cried the man, "she is the most beautiful creature I ever saw in my life."
> Lord Orville . . . laughed, but answered, "Yes, a pretty modest-looking girl."
> "O my Lord! . . . she is an angel!"
> "A *silent* one," returned he.
> "Why . . . she looks all intelligence and expression."
> "A poor weak girl!" answered Lord Orville, shaking his head.
>
> (39)

Orville's gentle disparagement becomes in Darcy supercilious conceit. Bingley, like Orville's interlocutor, praises the heroine—she is "very pretty, and I dare say very agreeable," he says. Darcy replies, "She is tolerable; but not handsome enough to tempt *me;* and I am in no humour at present to give consequence to young ladies who are slighted by other men" (12).

The scene in *Pride and Prejudice* where Sir William Lucas attempts to join Elizabeth's and Darcy's hands for a dance also seems to be a parody of an episode of *Evelina*. In Fanny Burney's novel Evelina attempts to avoid dancing with the rakish Sir Clement Willoughby, whom she dislikes, by pretending to be engaged to Lord Orville for the dance in question. Sir Clement, suspecting she is not being truthful, attempts to embarrass her by conducting her to Orville and presenting him with her hand. "He suddenly seized my hand," Evelina writes, "saying"

> "think, my Lord, what must be my reluctance to resign this fair hand to your Lordship!"

Literary Allusion

In the same instant, Lord Orville took it of him; I coloured
violently, and made an effort to recover it. "You do me too much
honour, Sir," cried he (with an air of gallantry, pressing it to his lips
before he let it go) "however, I shall be happy to profit by it . . . "
    To compel him thus to dance I could not endure, and eagerly
called out, "By no means,—not for the world!—I must beg—."
                                                            (51–52)

Orville's warm and lively gallantry becomes in *Pride and Prejudice*
Darcy's stiff propriety. (Although, by this time, he is "not unwilling"
to receive Elizabeth's hand, contrary to her opinion.) Sir William, we
remember, takes Elizabeth's hand and

> would have given it to Mr. Darcy . . . when (Elizabeth) instantly
> drew back, and said with some discomposure to Sir William.
>   "Indeed, Sir, I have not the least intention of dancing.—I en-
> treat you not to suppose that that I moved this way in order to beg
> for a partner."
>   Mr. Darcy with grave propriety requested to be allowed the
> honour of her hand; but in vain. (26)

The Darcy that we find in *Pride and Prejudice* is a very subtle,
rounded character, unlike the pasteboard creations that Austen created for parody in the juvenilia. I think, however, that he may very
well hark back to a prototype similar to the parody figures of her
earlier creations. If *Pride and Prejudice* developed, through revisions,
from a much earlier work, and much of the early work is parodic, is
it not likely that the prototype of *Pride and Prejudice* was a parody,
or contained a strong parodic element? Such a theory of Darcy's literary ancestry would account for a feature of *Pride and Prejudice* that
troubles a number of critics: the very great—for some readers improb-
ably great—difference between the Darcy we encounter in the early
part of the novel and the one we see at its conclusion. For some readers
the arrogance and conceit displayed in the ballroom scene or the proposal scene are so extreme that it is a bit difficult to believe that the
Darcy who displays them could ever turn into the properly humbled

man Elizabeth loves and marries. Is it possible that the early, trouble-some extremities of behavior and language are traces of an earlier, parodic figure similar to Charles Adams?

Leaving speculations as to its antecedents aside, the fact remains that *Pride and Prejudice,* as we have it today, is full of satiric allusion to the patrician hero motif. In addition to the treatment of Darcy, there are several other aspects of the novel that we should consider in this light. Darcy's relationship with Bingley is humorously reminiscent of Sir Charles Grandison's tendency to manage the lives of his friends. While Sir Charles manages upon request, and well, Darcy domineers over the too-pliant Bingley and at least temporarily maneuvers him away from his obvious soul mate, Jane Bennet. Miss Bingley is a nas-tily humorous version of the patrician hero's female adorers—praising, seeking his opinions, and so forth with ten thousand a year and Pem-berley in view. Most important, there is the role that Elizabeth Bennet plays in the novel's allusive pattern.

While Miss Bingley is an antitype in the sense that she is an ex-aggeration and distortion of qualities in the typical patrician hero's female adorers, Elizabeth is an anti-Evelina or -Harriet Byron in an-other way. That is to say, throughout the novel—or most of it at any rate—she acts in a way that is the opposite of that in which a Burney–Richardson heroine "ought" to behave. She will not "play her role." Instead of admiring Darcy's virtues, salivating over his beauty, ear-nestly seeking his advice, and treasuring up his every word, she dis-likes, teases, argues with, and rebukes him. "My behaviour to you," she remarks to him when they look back over the past at the conclu-sion of the story, "was at least always bordering on the uncivil, and I never spoke to you without rather wishing to give you pain than not" (380). She is unimpressed by his money and rank—or rather sees them, in her egalitarian fashion, as causes of arrogance, officiousness, and snobbery. While he is worrying about how to avoid encouraging her in vain hopes of matrimony, she is regarding him as "only the man who had made himself agreeable no where" (23). And when he does propose—she turns him down. Surely we are meant to see the first proposal scene as the putting down of the patrician hero. Elizabeth prefaces her refusal with a remark that would recall humorously to Austen's audience the swooning gratitude of an Evelina on receiving Orville's proposal. She is careful *not* to thank him for his attraction to her: "In such cases as these, it is, I believe, the established mode to express a sense of obligation for the sentiments avowed, however unequally they may be returned . . . and if I could *feel* gratitude, I would now thank you. But I cannot—I have never desired your good opinion, and you have certainly bestowed it most unwillingly" (190). And she proceeds to give him a tongue-lashing in which she accuses him of "arrogance" and "conceit," of officious interference in the affairs of Bingley and Jane, and of abusing the power his position gives him over the dependant Wickham. The patrician hero has been tumbled from his pedestal—with a vengeance.

But Austen manipulates the traditional motif in a still more complicated way. Once Darcy has been humbled, she turns her ironic attention to her anti-Evelina, Elizabeth. Elizabeth, as we have seen, learns that in her own pride and prejudice she has exaggerated Darcy's faults and failed to see much that is good in him. Reading Darcy's letter, she learns the truth about his relations with Wickham and is forced to admit that Darcy's understandable misreading of Jane's undemonstrative demeanor palliates to some extent his interference in the Jane–Bingley affair. Touring Pemberley she reflects on the positive aspects of his consciousness of social position. By the end of the book, although she can still laugh at certain aspects of her hero, Elizabeth is no longer quite the same as the woman who angrily refused to play Evelina to Darcy's Orville, Harriet Byron to his Sir Charles Grandison.

It is interesting to note, in this respect, that in the latter parts of *Pride and Prejudice* Austen ceases to create satiric parallels to the works of Richardson and Fanny Burney and even does a bit of what seems to be "straight" borrowing. At Pemberley, Darcy behaves with a marked tact toward the Gardiners and a gallantry toward Elizabeth that is really reminiscent of the Grandison–Orville manner. Again in patrician–heroic style he benevolently and efficiently exercises managerial talents, negotiating the difficult and unpleasant Lydia–Wickham affair, making suitable provisions for the couple, and preventing social disgrace to the Bennet family. He also nudges his friend Bingley back in the direction of Jane Bennet. Moreover, I believe that the early nineteenth-century audience would have recognized some specific "straight" echoes of *Sir Charles Grandison* in the "Pemberley" scenes of *Pride and Prejudice*. There is a marked resemblance between Pemberley, when Elizabeth visits it in the latter part of the novel, and the country residence of Sir Charles Grandison. Sir Charles is a most tasteful landscaper who "pretends not to level hills, or to force and distort nature; but to help it, as he finds it, without letting art be seen in his works, where he can possibly avoid it" (vol. 3, letter 23, 246). Thus, when Harriet visits his home she finds

> a large and convenient house . . . situated in a spacious park; which has several fine avenues leading to it.
>
> On the north side of the park flows a winding stream, that may well be called a river, abounding with trout and other fish; the current quickened by a noble cascade, which tumbles down its foaming waters from a rock, which is continued to some extent, in a ledge of rockwork, rudely disposed.
>
> The park is remarkable for its prospects, lawns, and rich-appearing clumps of trees of large growth. (vol. 6, letter 6, 30)

Compare the description of Darcy's Pemberley. The house, we are told, was

> situated on the opposite side of a valley, into which the road with some abruptness wound. It was a large, handsome, stone building, standing well on rising ground, and backed by a ridge of high woody hills;—and in front, a stream of some natural importance was swelled into greater, but without any artificial appearance. Its banks were neither formal, nor falsely adorned. Elizabeth was delighted. She had never seen a place for which nature had done more, or where natural beauty had been so little counteracted by an awkward taste. (245)

The emphasis on naturalness, the fine timber and good prospects, the trout stream artificially but discreetly improved—these, I think, are not accidental, especially in a piece of description most unusually detailed for the generally nonvisual Austen.

Both Harriet Byron and Elizabeth Bennet speak with elderly, respectable housekeepers in their tours of their heroes' houses; and both housekeepers sing their masters' praises, stressing their kindness to servants and tenants: "All his servants love him," Sir Charles's housekeeper says to Harriet, "indeed, we all adore him; and have prayed morning, noon and night for his coming hither, and settling among us" (vol. 7, letter 9, 52). Darcy's housekeeper describes him as "the best landlord, and the best master, that ever lived . . . There is not one of his tenants or servants but what will give him a good name" (249). Harriet and Elizabeth both visit picture galleries in their tours of the houses, and both are impressed by portraits of their heroes. By the end of her tour of Pemberley there is even a touch of Harriet-like gratitude in Elizabeth's mind as she thinks of Darcy's love for her. In a passage quoted earlier on Elizabeth's progress toward moral perceptiveness we are told that "as she stood before the canvas, on which he was represented, and fixed her eyes upon herself, she thought of his regard with a deeper sentiment of gratitude than it had ever raised before; she remembered its warmth, and softened its impropriety of expression" (251).

If one part of *Pride and Prejudice* is devoted to putting down the patrician hero, another is devoted to partially reinstating him. In a manner that reminds me of Pope's treatment of Belinda and her upperclass friends in *The Rape of the Lock,* Austen *both* pokes fun at and ultimately affirms the society figure with which she is concerned.

Thus, for the properly alerted reader, part of the fun of *Pride and Prejudice* consists in seeing it as a put-down of the patrician hero—a complicated, sophisticated put-down that turns upon itself toward the end for our additional delight. Moreover, just as do the other technical features of the novel that have been discussed in this study, the allusive pattern has another function. It complements—or rather, expresses in yet another way—the pattern of opposition followed by reconciliation that makes the novel "tick." Thematically, the book contrasts, in

Darcy and Elizabeth, sets of values identifiable in terms of the anti-thesis between art and nature in the comprehensive eighteenth-century senses of those terms. Self-knowledge, in each, brings modification of his or her extreme, and love between the two blends the modified opposites in a *concordia discors*. It is precisely this pattern that Austen's handling of the patrician hero motif follows. At the beginning of the novel a Burney–Richardson aristocrat of the stuffiest sort is challenged by an egalitarian revolutionary against the role of Evelina and Harriet Byron. He goes down in defeat—but only partly. She is victorious—but not entirely. The novel ends with marriage between a properly humbled patrician hero and a partial approximation to the patrician hero's usual heroine. We come once again to the matter of Austen's almost perfect artistic economy. Like everything else in *Pride and Prejudice* allusion "works" for its author thematically. Like everything else, it demonstrates the reasonableness of the nineteenth-century critic George Henry Lewes's opinion that Austen is "the greatest artist that has ever written, using the term to signify the most perfect mastery over the means to her end."

NOTES

1. For more detailed discussion on this subject see J. M. S. Tompkins, *The Popular Novel in England, 1770-1800*, chapter 8; chapter 6 of my own *Jane Austen's Art of Allusion* and Marilyn Butler, *Jane Austen and the War of Ideas*. Publication data on these works is given in the Bibliography.

2. For the fully developed presentation of ideas I am sketching here, see Ian Watt, *The Rise of the Novel: Studies in Defoe, Richardson and Fielding* (Berkeley: University of California Press, 1967).

3. *The English Novel: Form and Function* (New York: Harper & Row, 1961), 99. For reproductions of this essay, see the Bibliography.

4. "The Parallel of Deism and Classicism," *Modern Philology* 29 (1931–32):287–88.

5. E. M. W. Tillyard, *The Elizabethan World Picture* (London: Chatto & Windus, 1960), 77. I am very heavily indebted to Tillyard's work for this section of my chapter.

6. Samuel Kliger, "*Pride and Prejudice* in the Eighteenth-Century Mode," *University of Toronto Quarterly* 16 (1947):357–70. For reproductions of this excellent essay see the Bibliography.

7. For further discussion of this aspect of the book see Mordecai Marcus, "A Major Thematic Pattern in *Pride and Prejudice*," *Nineteenth Century Fiction* 16 (1961):274–79. Marcus's essay in reproduced in Elliot Rubenstein, *Twentieth Century Interpretations of "Pride and Prejudice*," cited in the Bibliography.

8. Adam Smith, *The Theory of Moral Sentiments* (London, 1802), 378. Subsequent page references are included in the text.

9. I am heavily indebted throughout the remainder of this chapter to the ground-breaking study of Howard S. Babb, *Jane Austen's Novels: The Fabric of Dialogue*. (See the Bibliography.)

10. Norman Page, *The Language of Jane Austen*, 54–55. (See the Bibliography.)

11. Austen develops her characters' verbal styles not only in their

speeches proper but also at times in "indirect speech," in which what are presented technically as narrative passages are colored by the linguistic peculiarities of the characters with whom they are concerned. One example of this is Mrs. Bennet's response to the second visit of Mr. Collins to Longbourn, after his engagement to Charlotte Lucas:

> Mr. Collins's return to Hertfordshire was no longer a matter of pleasure to Mrs. Bennet. On the contrary she was as much disposed to complain of it as her husband.—It was very strange that he should come to Longbourn instead of to Lucas Lodge; it was also very inconvenient and exceedingly troublesome.—She hated having visitors in the house when her health was so indifferent, and lovers were of all people the most disagreeable. Such were the gentle murmurs of Mrs. Bennet, and they gave way only to the greater distress of Mr. Bingley's continued absence. (128)

Although the excerpt is in the third person, sentences 3 and 4 clearly reproduce Mrs. Bennet's hyperbolic querulousness. Similarly, the opening part of the conversation of Mr. Collins with Mrs. Bennet referred to in chapter 8 of this study (pages 66–67 in the novel) is begun in narrative form but is heavily loaded with Collins's verbal mannerisms.

12. See my "The Balm of Sisterly Consolation," *Notes and Queries*, n.s. 30 (1983):216–17.

13. The borrowing is pointed out by F. W. Bradbrook in the Oxford English Novels edition of *Pride and Prejudice* (London: Oxford University Press, 1970), 350.

14. See my "The Olive Branch Metaphor in *Pride and Prejudice*," *Notes and Queries*, n.s. 30 (1983):214–15, and B. C. Southam, "Jane Austen and *Clarissa*," *Notes and Queries*, n.s. 10 (1963):191–92.

15. Samuel Richardson, *Sir Charles Grandison*, in *The Novels of Samuel Richardson* (London: Chapman & Hall, 1902), preface, x. All references will be to this edition.

16. Fanny Burney, *Evelina* (Garden City, N. Y.: Doubleday & Company, n.d.), 280. All references will be to this edition.

17. See my "Evelina in *Vanity Fair*: Becky Sharp and Her Patrician Heroes," *Nineteenth Century Fiction* 27 (1972):171–81.

18. E. E. Duncan-Jones makes this point in "Notes on Jane Austen," *Notes and Queries*, 196 (1951):14–16.

19. "A Critical Theory of Jane Austen's Writings, Part 1," *Scrutiny* 10 (1941):61–87.

BIBLIOGRAPHY

Primary Sources

Jane Austen

The standard edition of the fictional writings is the Oxford edition, which includes:

Sense and Sensibility. Edited and annotated by R. W. Chapman. Vol. 1. London: Oxford University Press, 1933. Includes notes on Austen's language.

Pride and Prejudice. Edited and annotated by R. W. Chapman. Vol. 2. London: Oxford University Press, 1933. Includes notes on the novel's relationship to Fanny Burney's *Cecilia* and on forms of address in Austen's novels.

Mansfield Park. Edited and annotated by R. W. Chapman. Vol. 3. London: Oxford University Press, 1933. Includes the text of the play *Lovers Vows,* which was performed in that novel.

Emma. Edited and annotated by R. W. Chapman. Vol. 4. London: Oxford University Press, 1933. Includes notes on eighteeneth-century manners and on punctuation in Austen's writing.

Northanger Abbey and *Persuasion.* Edited and annotated by R. W. Chapman. Vol. 5. London: Oxford University Press, 1933. Includes the "Biographical Notice" on Austen composed by her brother Henry.

Minor Works. Edited and annotated by R. W. Chapman. Vol. 6. London: Oxford University Press, 1954. Austen juvenilia and unfinished later work.

Jane Austen's "Sir Charles Grandison." Edited and annotated by B. C. Southam. Vol. 7. Oxford: Clarendon Press, 1980. A recently authenticated dramatic sketch based on Richardson's novel.

Most of Austen's surviving letters are collected, annotated and indexed in:

Jane Austen's Letters to Her Sister Cassandra and Others. Edited and annotated by R. W. Chapman. London: Oxford University Press, 1952.

Austen's Milieu (Works 1740–1813)

All of the following works, most certainly known to Austen, represent some of the more important aspects of her literary milieu. Editions and publishers are not specified; dates are those of the first publication. The readily accessible works, such as those by Sterne and Johnson, appear in many accurate and convenient editions.

Barrett, Eaton S. *The Heroine* (1813). A satire on the sentimental and Gothic fiction that Austen read and parodied. In fact, she is known to have read this work twice.

Burney, Fanny. *Evelina* (1778). Burney was one of Austen's favorite novelists.

———. *Cecilia* (1782).

———. *Camilla* (1796).

Cowper, William. *The Task* (1784). Cowper was a contemporary poet whom Austen much admired.

Crabbe, George. *The Borough* (1810). The contemporary poet Crabbe was also much admired by Austen.

Edgeworth, Maria. *Belinda* (1801).

———. *Tales of Fashionable Life* (first series, 1810; second series 1812).

Gisbourne, Thomas. *An Enquiry into the Duties of the Female Sex* (1798). A popular moral and educational work, probably referred to in one of Austen's letters.

Johnson, Samuel. *The Rambler* (1750–52). Essays. One of Austen's favorite writers, Johnson was referred to as her "dear Mr. Johnson."

———. *Rasselas* (1759). Didactic novel.

———. *Lives of the Poets* (1779–81). Biography and criticism.

Mackenzie, Henry. *The Man of Feeling* (1771). Representative of the excesses of the "sentimental" novels influenced by Sterne.

More, Hannah. *Strictures on the Modern System of Female Education* (1799). Advocating improved educational standards for women, this work probably influenced Austen's *Mansfield Park* specifically, and her thinking and writing in general.

———. *Coelebs in Search of a Wife* (1808). Didactic novel dramatizing the doctrines of the *Strictures*; mentioned in Austen's letters.

Radcliffe, Ann. *The Mysteries of Udolpho* (1794). Most famous example of the Gothic school of fiction that Austen often satirized.

———. *The Romance of the Forest* (1791). Gothic novel that Austen parodied in *Northanger Abbey* and alluded to in *Emma*.

Richardson, Samuel. *Pamela* (1740–41).

———. *Clarissa* (1747–48).

———. *Sir Charles Grandison* (1753–54).

Bibliography

Sterne, Lawrence. *A Sentimental Journey through France and Italy* (1768). Sterne's work was influential in establishing the hyperemotional, lachry- mose "sentimental novel" popular in the latter part of the eighteenth cen- tury and ridiculed by Austen in her juvenilia.

Secondary Sources

Bibliographies

Gilson, David. *A Bibliography of Jane Austen.* Oxford: Clarendon Press, 1982. Includes material on editions, translations, early reviews, and mod- ern scholarship up to 1978.

Roth, Barry, and Weinsheimer, Joel. *An Annotated Bibliography of Jane Aus- ten Studies, 1952–1972.* Charlottesville: University Press of Virginia, 1973.

Roth, Barry. *An Annotated Bibliography of Jane Austen Studies, 1973–1983.* Charlottesville: University Press of Virginia, 1985.

Biographies

Honan, Park. *Jane Austen. Her Life.* New York: St. Martin's Press, 1987. Illustrations, family trees, and notes are included.

Lascelles, Mary. *Jane Austen and Her Art,* see below.

Critical Studies

Babb, Howard. *Jane Austen's Novels: The Fabric of Dialogue.* Columbus: Ohio State University Press, 1962. An excellent study of one of Austen's most important technical features.

Bradbrook, F. W. *Jane Austen and Her Predecessors.* Cambridge: Cambridge University Press, 1966. Sound coverage of Austen's literary backgrounds of all sorts.

Burrows, J. F. *Computation into Criticism: A Study of Jane Austen's Novels and An Experiment in Method.* Oxford: Clarendon Press, 1987. Uses computer-based concordances and statistical analysis to generate data re- garding the thirty most commonly used words in Austen's dialogue. (That is, personal pronouns, articles, conjunctions, auxiliary verb forms, and the like: words such as "I," "a," "and," or "is".) The data generally confirm things established by critics such as Babb and Page on the basis of more "important" words and verbal constructions.

Butler, Marilyn. *Jane Austen and the War of Ideas.* Oxford: Clarendon Press, 1975. Historical study relating Austen to the "Jacobin" controversy of the late eighteenth and early nineteenth centuries.

Devlin, D. D. *Jane Austen and Education.* London: Macmillan Press, 1975. Material on educational theory likely to have influenced Austen.

Lascelles, Mary. *Jane Austen and Her Art.* London: Oxford University Press, 1939, 1963. An excellent biography and superb critical study.

Moler, Kenneth L. *Jane Austen's Art of Allusion.* Lincoln: University of Nebraska Press, 1968, 1977. Studies the six novels in relation to popular themes, character types, and situations from the literature best known to Austen.

Mudrick, Marvin. *Jane Austen: Irony as Defense and Discovery.* Princeton: Princeton University Press, 1953. A highly controversial work stressing the radical elements in Austen's social and moral thinking.

Page, Norman. *The Language of Jane Austen.* Oxford: Basil Blackwell, 1972. A somewhat more technical, useful complement to Babb's work on Austen's language.

Smith, Leroy W. *Jane Austen and the Drama of Women.* New York: St. Martin's Press, 1983. One of the best feminist readings of Austen.

Tompkins, J. M. S. *The Popular Novel in England, 1770–1800.* Lincoln: University of Nebraska Press, 1961. Valuable material on minor fiction of Austen's day, including summaries.

Articles and Chapters in Books

Brower, Reuben. "Light and Bright and Sparkling: Irony and Fiction in *Pride and Prejudice.*" In *The Fields of Light.* New York: Oxford University Press, 1951. Studies ambivalence in the dialogues between Elizabeth and Darcy in *Pride and Prejudice.* Reprinted in Booth, Gray, Heath, Southam, and Watt (see Collections of Essays below).

Harding, D. W. "Regulated Hatred: An Aspect of the Work of Jane Austen." *Scrutiny* 8 (1940):346–62. A precursor of the "radical" interpretations of Austen associated with Mudrick and others. Reprinted in Heath, Watt.

Kliger, Samuel. "*Pride and Prejudice* in the Eighteenth-Century Mode." *University of Toronto Quarterly* 16 (1947):357–70. A reading of the novel in terms of the eighteenth-century "art-nature" antithesis. Reprinted in Gray, Rubinstein.

Bibliography

Lewis, C. S. "A Note on Jane Austen." *Essays in Criticism* 4 (1954):359–71. The "self-knowledge" theme in *Northanger Abbey, Sense and Sensibility,* and *Pride and Prejudice.* Reprinted in Heath, Watt.

Van Ghent, Dorothy. "On *Pride and Prejudice.*" In *The English Novel: Form and Function.* New York: Holt, Rinehart & Winston, 1953. The relationship of the individual and society in the novel. Reprinted in Booth, Rubinstein.

Collections Especially Relevant to *Pride and Prejudice*

Booth, Bradford A. *Pride and Prejudice.* New York: Harcourt, Brace & World, 1963.

Gray, Donald J. *Pride and Prejudice.* New York: Norton & Company, 1966.

Heath, William. *Discussions of Jane Austen.* Boston: D. C. Heath & Co., 1961.

Rubinstein, Elliot L. *Twentieth Century Interpretations of "Pride and Prejudice": A Collection of Critical Essays.* Englewood Cliffs: Prentice-Hall, 1969.

Southam, B. C. *"Sense and Sensibility," "Pride and Prejudice" and "Mansfield Park": A Casebook.* London: Macmillan Press, 1976.

Watt, Ian. *Jane Austen: A Collection of Critical Essays.* Englewood Cliffs: Prentice-Hall, 1963.

INDEX ———

Anti-Jacobin Review, 2
Austen, Jane, *Letters,* 67, 68; *Minor Works,* 29, 81–83, 91–92
Austen-Leigh, James Edward, 10

Babb, Howard, 12
Berkeley, George, 85
Blackwood's Magazine, 9
Boswell, James, 86
Bradbrook, F. W., 12
Brower, Reuben, 11–12
Burney, Fanny, 84; *Evelina,* as source for prominent motif, 89–91; specific scenes from *Evelina* burlesqued, 93–95
Butler, Marilyn, 11
Byron, George, 81

Cecil, David, 10
Chapman, R. W., 10, 86
Coleridge, Samuel, 1
Cooper, Edward, 84

Devlin, D. D., 11
Dryden, John, 19, 39
Duckworth, Alaistair, 11

Eliot, George, *Adam Bede,* 63–64

Fielding, Henry, 3–4, 19, 40
Forster, E. M., 10
Fowler, Margaret, 12

Gisbourne, Thomas, 29
Godwin, William, 2
Golding, William, 20
Goldsmith, Oliver, 81

Hamilton, Elizabeth, 2
Harding, D. W., 10
Hays, Mary, 2
Hull, Thomas, 91
Hume, David, 29, 85

Johnson, Samuel, 19, 29, 49, 66; as quoted in Boswell, 86

Kirkham, Margaret, 12
Kliger, Samuel, 11, 43
Koppel, Gene, 13

Lascelles, Mary, 10
Leavis, Q. D., 12, 93–95
Lewes, George Henry, 9
Litz, Walton, 11
Lovejoy, A. O., 18

Mason, John, 29, 34
Moler, Kenneth, 11, 12
Monaghan, David, 12
More, Hannah, 2, 29, 81
Mudrick, Marvin, 10–11

North British Review, 9

Page, Norman, 12, 69
Persuasions, 13

Index

Pope, Alexander, 19, 38–40, 66–67
Porter, Anna Maria, 91

Quarterly Review, 8–9

Richardson, Samuel, 3–4, 19, 87;
  Sir Charles Grandson as source of
  a prominent motif, 87–89;
  specific scenes echoed, 97–99
Rousseau, Jean-Jacques, 2

Scott, Walter, 8–9
Simpson, Richard, 9
Smith, Adam, 58–59, 85

Smith, Leroy, 12
Swift, Jonathan, 19

Tave, Stuart, 11
Ten Harmsel, Henrietta, 12
Tillyard, E. M. W., 35–37

Van Ghent, Dorothy, 11, 18

Watt, Ian, 3
Westminster Review, 9
Whately, Richard, 9
Wollstonecraft, Mary, 2
Woolf, Virginia, 10
Wordsworth, William, 1

ABOUT THE AUTHOR ———

Kenneth L. Moler was born in Baltimore in 1938 and attended the college preparatory course of The Baltimore City College. He received his B.A. from Johns Hopkins University in 1958 and was awarded a Woodrow Wilson Fellowship to Harvard University. After serving in the U. S. Army Ordnance Corps at Aberdeen Proving Ground, Maryland, he received his M.A. and Ph.D. degrees from Harvard University, completing a doctoral dissertation on Jane Austen. He has taught at Harvard and at the University of Nebraska-Lincoln, where he is currently professor of English. His specialties in literature are Austen, eighteenth- and early nineteenth-century fiction, and eighteenth-century poetry.

Professor Moler has published numerous scholarly articles on Austen and other eighteenth- and nineteenth-century figures in American, British, and European journals. In 1976 he was chosen, as one of eighteen of the most distinguished contemporary scholars on Austen, to contribute an essay to the Cambridge University Press's Austen bicentennial volume, *Jane Austen: Bicentenary Essays*. His book-length critical study of Austen's relationship to the literary traditions of her day, *Jane Austen's Art of Allusion,* is kept permanently in print in the University of Nebraska Press's Landmark Edition Series. Professor Moler is a member of the board of patrons of the Jane Austen Society of North America, serves as an editorial consultant on eighteenth-century fiction for several university presses, and reviews for the *Eighteenth Century: A Current Biography.*